Designing
Expert Systems

Designing
Expert Systems

A Guide to Selecting Implementation Techniques

Paul J. Kline

Steven B. Dolins

Texas Instruments
Dallas, Texas

WILEY

JOHN WILEY & SONS

NEW YORK • CHICHESTER • BRISBANE • TORONTO • SINGAPORE

Library of Congress Cataloging in Publication Data:

Kline, Paul J.
    Designing expert systems.

    Bibliography: p.
    Includes index.
    1. Expert systems (Computer science)   2. System
design.   I. Dolins, Steven B.   II. Title.
QA76.76.E95K54   1989   006.3'3   88-37869
ISBN 0-471-50484-X

Printed in the United States of America

10 9 8 7 6 5 4 3 2 1

To our parents

Joseph and Irene Kline
Max and Roslyn Dolins

Contents

Headings in italics denote Design Guidelines.

9   Future Applications of Design Guidelines   173

List of Figures

List of Tables

Preface

There is currently a great deal of excitement about the prospects for building new types of computer programs called *expert systems*. While it has long been accepted that computer programs can automate computational and clerical tasks, only with the advent of expert systems has it become possible to automate certain tasks requiring expert knowledge. The expertise of skilled physicians, troubleshooters, designers, analysts, and equipment operators are now being tapped to build expert systems to perform tasks of economic and scientific importance.

The automation of these tasks typically confers a variety of benefits:

- Proliferation of scarce expertise
- Consistent and reliable application of expertise
- Documentation of scarce knowledge

The recent emergence of a variety of software products for expert-system construction has provided widespread access to many of the tools and techniques needed to build expert systems. What is much less widespread is knowledge of how to design expert systems.

This book was written to try to help remedy that problem by providing guidelines that relate problem features to expert-system designs. These guidelines assist expert-system builders in choosing the right expert-system design and the right artificial intelligence (AI) techniques to solve the problem at hand. Since expert-system problems can differ rather dramatically, the guidelines should be useful for designers building their first expert-system or their twenty-first.

Even the experienced expert-system builder who needs no help in developing effective designs for expert systems may find it valuable to have a published source of design guidelines to refer to in design reviews or customer briefings.

We developed the guidelines primarily to assist the practitioner, that is, the expert-system designer. However, the use of quotations from the published literature on expert systems to support the guidelines also makes the book valuable to students of artificial intelligence. This book brings together in one place a wealth of insight and discussion that would otherwise require an extensive study of the professional literature on expert systems.

This discussion of expert systems provides one assessment of the current state of the art in this particular area of artificial intelligence:

- The techniques that have been developed
- The problems those techniques solve
- The pitfalls that might be encountered in using the techniques

We feel fortunate to have been able to collect and record some of the first steps taken in the direction of changing the design of expert systems from an art into a science.

PAUL J. KLINE
STEVEN B. DOLINS

Dallas, Texas
April 1989

Acknowledgments

The research for this book was supported by the Air Force Systems Command, Rome Air Development Center, Griffiss AFB, New York 13441 under contract no. F30602-83-C-0123. This book incorporates a large amount of the material that appeared in the final report of that contract. The preparation of this book was made possible by Texas Instruments Incorporated and its management, who assisted us in numerous ways.

We would like to thank Dr. Northrup Fowler III of Rome Air Development Center for his valuable suggestions during the course of this research. We are very grateful to the expert-system builders who were kind enough to comment on earlier versions of the guidelines: Bruce Buchanan, Penny Nii, Ruven Brooks, John Kunz, Bruce Porter, Robert Drazovich, Frederick Hayes-Roth, Robert Neches, Tim Finin, and Jim Kornell. They are, of course, in no way responsible for any deficiencies of the current set of guidelines.

We would also like to thank the following individuals for their assistance: Byron Davies, Tom Ekberg, Jim Bender, Ken Hill, and Gary Honeycutt at Texas Instruments and Diane Cerra and Wanda Cuevas at John Wiley & Sons.

We are very grateful to the publishers and authors who allowed us to reprint selections from their publications in this book. Rather than acknowledging all the copyright holders here, their names accompany reprinted materials throughout the book.

PAUL J. KLINE
STEVEN B. DOLINS

1 Introduction

A large number of decisions must be made in designing an expert system. For example:

- What knowledge representation technique should be used?
- What problem-solving strategy should be employed?
- How should uncertainty be handled?

Making the right decisions greatly simplifies the development of an expert system and helps to ensure its lasting usefulness. The goal of this book is to help expert-system builders make intelligent design decisions.

Before beginning, it is worth considering the difficulty of making expert-system design decisions: How difficult is it to select the proper artificial intelligence (AI) methods for a particular task? A recent paper by John McDermott, the developer of some of the most successful expert systems ever built, provides an answer:

> Although efforts, some successful, to develop expert systems (application systems that can perform knowledge-intensive tasks) have been going on now for almost 20 years, we are not yet very good at describing the variations in problem-solving methods that these systems use, nor do we have much of an understanding of how to characterize the methods in terms of features of the types of tasks for which they are appropriate [J. McDermott 1988, p. 225].

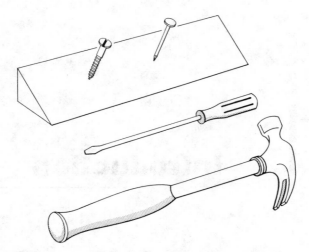

Figure 1.1. It is easy to select the right tool for driving nails and screws. Expert-system development software is often referred to as *toolkits*, which suggests, incorrectly, that it is easy to choose the right AI tool to solve an expert-system design problem.

Despite McDermott's suggestion that it can be difficult to make design decisions, it would be possible for the casual observer to get the impression that it is easy to select the appropriate AI technique to solve a particular problem. For example, the vendors of software systems that support the construction of expert systems often refer to their products as "toolkits." The use of the word "toolkit" to describe this software conjures up images of hammers, screwdrivers, saws, and similar hardware items. The implied suggestion is that selecting the right AI tool for an expert-system problem is roughly as difficult as deciding whether a hammer, screwdriver, or saw is the right tool for a particular repair job. As suggested by Figure 1.1, selecting the appropriate household tool is often easy. Even without experience with these two tools, it is easy to see that the hammer is the right tool for driving the nail and the screwdriver the right tool for driving the screw.

Unfortunately, the task facing the expert-system builder is considerably more difficult than this analogy to selecting real tools suggests. A better analogy is the problem of selecting the appropriate household chemicals to solve cleaning and stain-removal problems. Figure 1.2 offers two alternatives for removing stains, rust stains in one case and mustard stains in the other. *Hints from Heloise* [1980, pp. 380f.] provides the right answer: The lemon juice will remove the rust stains and the vinegar will remove the mustard stains. (In case the correct answer

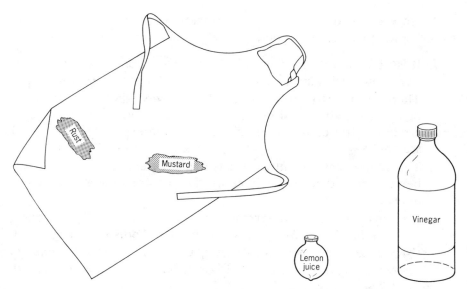

Figure 1.2. Selecting the right household chemical to remove rust stains and mustard stains is harder than the hammer–screwdriver problem depicted in Figure 1.1. Choosing the right AI technique to solve an expert-system problem is more like this stain-removal problem.

to this problem is obvious, perhaps you can also explain why Heloise provides the stern warning "Never use ammonia" to try to remove a mustard stain.)

It is not easy to guess that lemon juice is effective for removing rust stains and vinegar for removing mustard stains, even with a lifetime of familiarity with these chemicals. The fact that there are many such "nonobvious" tools for cleaning has kept Heloise busy for many years churning out household hints.

One way to view this book is as a version of *Hints from Heloise* for the expert-system builder. Simply knowing about Rule interpreters, Frame systems, and Blackboard systems does not guarantee that it is easy to see which of these should be used for a particular expert-system problem—no more than knowing about vinegar and lemon juice guarantees that it is easy to see which of them should be used on the stains.

The examination of the design guidelines for building expert systems found in Chapters 2 through 7 of this book supports the argument that selecting the right AI technique to solve a problem is more like choosing the right stain remover than it is like choosing the right tool from a toolbox.

There are a number of reasons why now is a good time to define expert-system design guidelines:

1. It is possible to formulate reliable advice. Enough expert systems have now been built to support some useful generalizations.
2. There are many people who need the advice. Expert systems are being built today in large numbers, and in many cases the designers have little or no experience in building expert systems or AI systems.
3. The advice that currently exists is not sufficient. There are a number of books that offer advice on the construction of expert systems. For example:
   (a) Hayes-Roth, F., Waterman, D. A., and Lenat, D. B. (eds.), *Building Expert Systems*. Reading, MA: Addison-Wesley, 1983.
   (b) Weiss, S. M., and Kulikowski, C. A., *A Practical Guide to Designing Expert Systems*. Totowa, NJ: Rowman & Allanheld, 1984.
   (c) Buchanan, B. G., and Shortliffe, E. H. (eds.), *Rule-Based Expert Systems: The MYCIN Experiments of the Stanford Heuristic Programming Project*. Reading, MA: Addison-Wesley, 1984.
   (d) Waterman, D. A., *A Guide to Expert Systems*. Reading, MA: Addison-Wesley, 1986.
   (e) Walters, J. R., and Nielsen, N. R., *Crafting Knowledge-Based Systems: Expert Systems Made ~~Easy~~ Realistic*. New York: Wiley-Interscience, 1988.

   While each of these books is quite useful in its own sphere, even taken together they do not provide a fully adequate set of design guidelines.
4. Constructing the advice promises to contribute to the development of AI. Artificial Intelligence researchers have focused more attention on developing new techniques and tools than on characterizing the usefulness of the techniques that already exist. A clear appreciation of the range of usefulness of existing techniques should contribute to the future development of the field.

1.1 ORGANIZATION OF THIS BOOK

Chapters 2 through 7 each contain a set of design guidelines for building expert systems. An example of a design guideline is presented in Section 1.1.1. All the other design guidelines have similar formats.

In this example, the guideline, which is shown in boldface type, poses questions regarding the signal-to-noise (S/N) ratio of the input data in the problem that the expert-system builder hopes to solve with an expert system. If there is a low S/N ratio in this problem, Model-Driven Reasoning is the recommended AI technique. Data-Driven Reasoning is recommended when there is a high S/N ratio. In this example, the expert-system builder or knowledge engineer would most likely be able to determine the S/N ratio by interviewing domain experts and asking them specifically about this issue. To follow the advice of other guidelines it might be necessary to analyze the way domain experts solve example problems instead of asking them directly.

1.1.1 Example Guideline: Signal-to-Noise Ratio

Will the expert system be solving a signal-interpretation problem?

and

Is it hard to distinguish true signals from noise (i.e., low S/N ratio)?

or

Is it easy to distinguish true signals from noise (i.e., high S/N ratio)?

Evidence: Any   Type: Preenumerated, constructed

Low S/N ratio → *Model-Driven Reasoning*

Evidence: Weak, moderate

High S/N ratio → *Data-Driven Reasoning*

Evidence: Moderate, powerful

Section 1.2 will explain how the notation

Evidence: Any   Type: Preenumerated, constructed

is used to indicate the range of problems for which it is reasonable to apply this guideline regarding S/N ratios. That section will also discuss how the notations following the answers can be used to determine some of the characteristics of the problem under discussion.

The reader may be interested in knowing why a low S/N ratio implies Model-Driven Reasoning. Following the guideline and the recommended AI techniques are supporting arguments for those recommendations. These justifications typically take the form of quotations from the published literature on expert systems. For Guideline 1.1.1 the justification includes the quote shown in Section 1.1.2 from a paper describing the HASP/SIAP expert system.

There are two advantages of using quotations in supporting arguments for the design guidelines in this book:

1. The quotations help ensure that the design guidelines have some degree of support among expert-system builders, as opposed to merely reflecting the personal biases of the authors of this book.
2. The quotations provide pointers to additional sources of information on a particular issue.

1.1.2   Support for Example Guideline 1.1.1

The following quote is from a paper that describes the HASP/SIAP system for determining ship movements based on data from underwater acoustic sensors. As the following quote suggests, expectations derived from a model can be used to help distinguish signals from noise in domains where noise is a problem. In the HASP/SIAP expert system these expectations can be derived from general knowledge about the location of shipping lanes and specific knowledge about recent ship positions. In domains that do not suffer from noise, the data can be taken at face value and there is much less chance of wasted effort or mistaken hypotheses when the data are used to propose hypotheses directly. Since Data-Driven Reasoning is easily misled by erroneous data, there would have to be a very high S/N ratio before it would be wise to rely completely on Data-Driven Reasoning without any support from expectations derived from other sources.

> Our experience points strongly toward the use of a combination of these techniques; some KS's [Knowledge Sources] are strongly data dependent while others are strongly model dependent. In HASP/SIAP the majority of the inferences are data-driven, with occasional model-driven inferences. The following are the guidelines we have used in the past to determine which of the two methods is more appropriate:

1. *Signal-to-noise ratio.* Problems which have inherently low S/N ratios are better suited to solutions by model-driven programs; the converse is true for problems with high S/N ratios.

2. *Availability of a model.* A model, sometimes referred to as *the semantics of the task domain*, can be used in various ways: (a) as input at some level of the hypothesis structure, (b) to make inferences based on general knowledge about the task domain, or (c) to make inferences based on specific knowledge about the particular task. In HASP/SIAP, the model is drawn from general knowledge about the signal sources and from external reports that serve to define the context. If a reliable model is available, the data-interpretation KSs can be used as *verifiers* rather than *generators* of inferences; this reduces the computational burden on the signal-processing programs at the "front end" [Nii, Feigenbaum, Anton, and Rockmore, 1982].
— Reprinted with permission from *AI Magazine*, 1982, p. 35, published by the American Association for Artificial Intelligence.

Since quotes are used extensively in this book, it should be made clear that the policy regarding quotations is to reproduce the original as closely as possible. For example, italic type is used in Section 1.1.2 only in the places that the original authors used it. That is, fonts have not been changed to add emphasis. Similarly, all the footnotes appearing in this book are reproductions of footnotes in the originals—footnotes are not used to comment on quoted materials. Any additions or elaborations made to the quotes are indicated by the use of square brackets, that is, "[...]."

The design guideline in Section 1.1.1 is obviously derived directly from the supporting quotation in Section 1.1.2. In other cases, the connection is considerably more indirect. The guidelines are not intended to be mere paraphrases of supporting quotations; rather, the quotes were used as a source of data in developing the guidelines. Having the quotes available makes it possible for readers to decide that they would prefer to draw an alternative conclusion from the same data.

The design guidelines in this book recommend a variety of AI techniques. These recommendations often need to be tempered by a discussion of the potential pitfalls associated with a technique. For example, Model-Driven Reasoning was the technique recommended in Guideline 1.1.1 if there was a low S/N ratio in the data. A pitfall of Model-Driven Reasoning is discussed in Section 1.1.3. Unless precautions are taken, Model-Driven Reasoning will see in the data what the model leads it to expect, regardless of what is really there.

1.1.3 Example Pitfall: Model-Driven Reasoning

Model-Driven Reasoning (also known as *Expectation-Driven Reasoning***)**

   has the problem

that it is prone to seeing whatever the model expects, regardless of what is really there.

> However, designers should beware that the model-driven approach is prone to "finding what is being looked for." Model-driven approaches should be supplemented with strong verification heuristics. [Nii, Feigenbaum, Anton, and Rockmore, 1982].
> — Reprinted with permission from *AI Magazine*, 1982, p. 35, published by the American Association for Artificial Intelligence.

Although this pitfall of Model-Based Reasoning is unfortunate, it is not necessarily fatal. By adding provisions in the expert-system design for carefully cross-checking the model's expectations against other information, this pitfall of Model-Based Reasoning can be overcome. Pitfalls of other recommended AI techniques are discussed in Chapter 8. Chapter 8 also recommends AI techniques to overcome some of these pitfalls.

   Artificial Intelligence implementation techniques are not the only tools that must be recommended with certain reservations and cautions. Similar cautions are found in *Hints from Heloise*. For example, Heloise recommends using dishwasher detergent for cleaning the porcelain enamel surfaces of bathtubs and sinks. Heloise warns that dishwasher detergent is very hard on the hands, so rubber gloves should be worn when using it. The intelligent use of tools of all kinds requires knowledge of the characteristic pitfalls of those tools.

   Chapter 9 describes some of the ways that design guidelines may be employed in building expert systems in the future. Appendix A provides a glossary to briefly describe some of the implementation techniques recommended in this book.

1.2 LOCATING THE RELEVANT GUIDELINES

Expert systems have been built for a wide variety of problems. Design guidelines that make perfect sense in reference to one of these problems make little or no sense in reference to another problem. In many cases, the arguments regarding design choices in the published literature implicitly assume a particular universe of problem types as the context for their remarks.

One way to deal with this problem is to add clauses to the guidelines that restrict them to the appropriate set of problems. The example design guideline concerning S/N ratios that was shown in Section 1.1.1 used the clause

Will the expert system be solving a signal-interpretation problem?

to ensure that the clause

Is it hard to distinguish true signals from noise (i.e., low S/N ratio)?

would be a meaningful question about the problem under discussion.

Such "screening clauses" are used with some frequency throughout this book. However, it becomes cumbersome to include all the required screening clauses to ensure that each guideline is applied in a meaningful way to all the diverse problems that might be solved by an expert system. The solution that has been adopted is to define two characteristics that distinguish a large number of problems and then index guidelines according to the values they assume for these characteristics: (1) the power of the available evidence and (2) the type of solution required. For example, the guideline in Section 1.1.1 included the line

Evidence: Any   Type: Preenumerated, constructed

This notation refers to the characteristics that describe the rows and columns of Table 1.1. The rows of this table describe the ability of the data available in a problem to unambiguously confirm or reject hypotheses. For example, the DENDRAL system [Buchanan, Sutherland, and Feigenbaum, 1970] identifies molecular compounds from chemical analysis data. Since DENDRAL can use these data with relative certainty to reject candidate molecular fragments, DENDRAL is placed in the "Powerful Evidence" row of Table 1.1.

When the problem is to diagnose infectious agents, however, the medical data does not have the same kind of power to confirm or reject hypothesized disease agents. Thus the MYCIN expert system [Buchanan and Shortliffe 1984] is frequently forced to rely on a weaker kind of evidence such as "*A suggests B*" or "*C and D tend* to rule out *E.*" The need to rely on this weaker evidence is the reason for placing MYCIN in the "Weak Evidence" row of Table 1.1.

	R1	SYN
Powerful Evidence	PUFF	DENDRAL	EL
		MOLGEN	DART
Moderate-Strength Evidence	MUD	HASP/SIAP	ABEL
	VM	CASNET	ISIS
Weak Evidence	MYCIN	INTERNIST	AM
	PROSPECTOR	HEARSAY-II	
	Preenumerated Solutions	Constructed Solutions	Symbolic Simulation

TABLE 1.1 The problems solved by expert systems can be categorized by the strength of the available evidence (rows of the table) and the way solutions are developed (columns of the table). The problems solved by some of the expert systems referred to in this book are categorized according to these dimensions.

The columns of Table 1.1 are labeled with three general categories of problems. For example, diagnosis tasks are often attacked by determining which of a preenumerated set of underlying causes are favored by the evidence. For this reason, MYCIN, which operates with a preenumerated set of disease hypotheses, is placed in the "Preenumerated Solutions" column of Table 1.1.

In the VAX configuration problem solved by R1 [McDermott, J. 1982], there are so many possible configurations that it is impractical to preenumerate them. Because R1 constructs a configuration for a VAX system out of individual components, it is placed in the "Constructed Solutions" column of Table 1.1.

Finally, solving a problem may rely on a symbolic simulation of a complex system to estimate the probable outcome of a set of design decisions (in SYN's circuit-design problem [Sussman and Steele 1980]), or the probable outcome of component failures (in EL's circuit-diagnosis problem [Stallman and Sussman 1977]). Given this understanding of the categories in Table 1.1, the notation

Evidence: Any   Type: Preenumerated, constructed

	Preenumerated Solutions	Constructed Solutions		Symbolic Simulation
Powerful Evidence	1.1.1 2.4 2.6 5.2 5.4 5.5	1.1.1 2.4 2.5 2.7 2.9 3.3 3.4 3.7	4.2 5.1 5.2 5.4 5.5 6.6 6.7 7.5	2.4 2.5 2.7 3.2 3.5 3.7 7.5
Moderate-Strength Evidence	1.1.1 2.4 2.6 2.8 3.2 5.2 5.4 5.5	1.1.1 2.4 2.5 2.7 2.8 2.9 3.2 3.3 3.4	3.7 3.8 4.2 5.1 5.2 5.4 5.5 6.6 6.7 7.5	2.4 2.5 2.7 3.2 3.5 3.7 3.8 7.5
Weak Evidence	1.1.1 2.7 2.8 3.2 5.2 5.4 5.5	1.1.1 2.5 2.5 2.8 3.2 3.3 3.4 3.7	3.8 4.2 5.1 5.2 5.4 5.5 6.6 6.7 7.5	2.5 2.7 3.2 3.5 3.7 3.8 7.5

TABLE 1.2   The numbers in each of the nine cells in this table are design guideline numbers. The design guidelines associated with cell (i, j) are the guidelines relevant to problems characterized by strength of evidence i and solution type j.

indicates that it is reasonable to apply Guideline 1.1.1, regarding S/N ratios, to problems with preenumerated solutions or problems with constructed solutions. Within this range, the guideline is sensible no matter how powerful the evidence.

The appropriate range of application of Guideline 1.1.1 is summarized in Table 1.2 by including the number 1.1.1 corresponding to Guideline 1.1.1 in all three cells in the "Preenumerated Solutions" column and all three cells in the "Constructed Solutions" column. Table 1.2 provides a quick way of indexing the set of design guidelines in this book. If the expert-system builder can estimate where a problem lies with respect to the categories of Table 1.2, then the entries in the table indicate which design guidelines in this book are particularly relevant to that problem. The numbers in Table 1.2 are all guideline numbers, and the table of contents can be consulted to locate the guidelines mentioned.

If a particular guideline makes sense for all three qualities of evidence and all three problem types, then the number of this guideline could have been listed in all nine cells of Table 1.2. However, since this book has many guidelines that are appropriate for all nine cells, Table 1.2 would have been very crowded. Instead, a separate table (Table 1.3) shows the numbers of the guidelines that are applicable for all combinations of strength of evidence and solution type. In Chapters 2 through 7, the notation

> Evidence: Any   Type: Any

is used to indicate that a guideline is not restricted to a particular subregion of Table 1.1. Since it is possible to index the correct cells of Table 1.2 only when the problem can be categorized properly, some of the guidelines try to offer assistance with this categorization. For example, Guideline 1.1.1 makes the following recommendations:

Low S/N ratio   → *Model-Driven Reasoning*

> Evidence: Weak, moderate

High S/N ratio   → *Data-Driven Reasoning*

> Evidence: Moderate, powerful

In addition to recommending Model-Driven Reasoning as an implementation technique, a low S/N ratio also implies that there is relatively weak evidence available in this problem. Thus the notation

> Evidence: Weak, moderate

2.1	4.1	4.7	6.3	7.2
2.2	4.3	4.8	6.4	7.3
2.3	4.4	5.3	6.5	7.4
3.1	4.5	6.1	6.8	7.6
3.6	4.6	6.2	7.1	7.7

TABLE 1.3 These guidelines are relevant to all nine cells in Table 1.2 because they are applicable to all evidence strengths and all solution types.

follows Model-Driven Reasoning to indicate that the problem in question must lie in the "Weak Evidence" or "Moderate-Strength Evidence" rows of Table 1.1. Characterization of the problem in this way helps to define what other guidelines might be relevant. However, a high S/N ratio suggests that relatively powerful evidence is available for this problem. Therefore, the high S/N answer includes the notation

Evidence: Moderate, powerful

indicating that the problem in question must lie in the "Moderate-Strength Evidence" or "Powerful Evidence" rows of Table 1.1.

1.2.1 Using Problem Characteristics to Index Design Guidelines

Figure 1.3 indicates how an expert-system builder with a particular problem in mind can use Tables 1.2 and 1.3 to determine which of the design guidelines in this book to consult. The following steps provide a systematic way to find the relevant guidelines:

1. First consult the guidelines in Table 1.3, as these guidelines are appropriate for a wide range of evidence types and solution types. The table of contents can be used to locate these guidelines. Alternatively, the text can be skimmed looking for guidelines with the notation

Evidence: Any   Type: Any

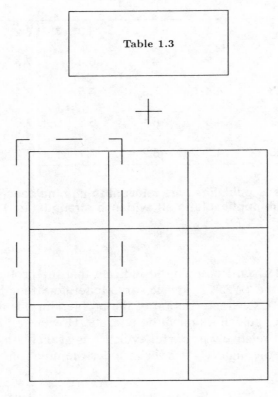

Table 1.2

Figure 1.3. Tables 1.2 and 1.3 can be used to find the design guidelines appropriate for solving a particular problem. Guideline numbers found in Table 1.3 are appropriate for a wide range of problems. The guidelines in Table 1.2 can be indexed by evidence strength and solution type.

2. In the process of consulting these guidelines, the recommendations will generally indicate where the problem in question lies with respect to the evidence strength categories and the solution-type categories. The expert-system builder is also likely to have intuitions about how these categories apply to that problem.

3. Use Table 1.2 to find additional guidelines that apply to the evidence strength(s) and solution type(s) that characterize the problem. In Figure 1.3 the dashed lines indicate that guidelines from two cells of Table 1.2 might be consulted in addition to the guidelines presented in Table 1.3.

1.2.2 Using Problem Characteristics to Index Implementation Techniques

We have seen that both guidelines and implementation techniques can be associated with subregions of Table 1.1. The example design guideline in Section 1.1.1 is applicable if the problem under discussion falls in the "Preenumerated Solutions" or "Constructed Solutions" columns of Table 1.1. Model-Driven Reasoning may be an appropriate implementation technique if the problem falls in the "Weak Evidence" or "Moderate-Strength Evidence" rows of Table 1.1. Data-Driven Reasoning may be an appropriate implementation technique if the problem falls in the "Moderate-Strength Evidence" or "Powerful Evidence" rows of Table 1.1.

Figure 1.4 provides a summary of some of the implementation techniques recommended in this book and their associated regions of application. In Figure 1.4, "Model-Driven Reasoning" is located near the "Weak Evidence" end and "Forward-Chaining," a synonym for "Data-Driven Reasoning," is placed closer to the "Powerful Evidence" end. A number of techniques recommended in this book are not listed in Figure 1.4 because they are not limited in applicability to a subregion of this table. That is, problem features other than strength of evidence and type of solution determine the applicability of these techniques.

An expert-system builder with a particular problem in mind can use Figure 1.4 to quickly determine a few of the AI implementation techniques discussed in this book that may be useful for solving that problem. The index can then be consulted to find where those techniques are discussed.

1.3 CAUTIONS IN USING THE GUIDELINES

One difficulty that arises in applying the design guidelines in this book is that sometimes a case can be made for more than one of the alternatives discussed in a particular design guideline. In other cases, two different guidelines appear to offer conflicting advice. There are at least two possible explanations:

1. The alternatives described in the guidelines might not be mutually exclusive, strictly speaking. In this case, it may be possible for several design recommendations to all be equally applicable to one and the same problem.

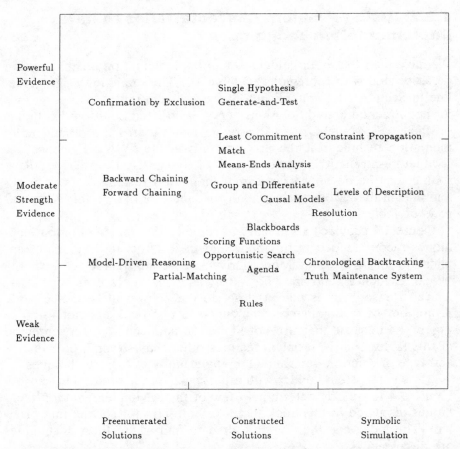

Figure 1.4. Some of the AI techniques recommended in this book are appropriate for only certain combinations of evidence characteristics and solution characteristics. The location of techniques in this figure provides a rough indication of where they are appropriate.

2. The alternatives cannot both be true of the same aspect of the problem, but the problem has several different aspects or subproblems. One design recommendation legitimately applies to one subproblem, and another design recommendation legitimately applies to a different subproblem.

In the first case, judgment is required to decide whether it is feasible to follow both recommendations in the same design. In the second case, judgment is required to decide whether the subproblems differ sufficiently to warrant receiving different designs. Unfortunately, it is not clear how to offer any general advice for dealing with these cases.

It is also possible that the techniques recommended by a design guideline are not the only techniques that address those problem features. While relevant techniques have not been intentionally omitted, it is likely that some possibly relevant techniques have been overlooked. For this reason, the reader is advised not to read too much into the omission of a technique from the recommendations of a guideline.

Another erroneous impression that could be conveyed by the design guidelines is that there are implementation techniques currently available to solve all the problems that arise in building expert systems. This is far from the truth, of course. There are many recognized limitations in the current expert-system technology. For example, there is a strong need for mechanisms that allow expert systems to reason about time.

It would be possible to include guidelines of the following form:

If a problem has $\rightarrow$ there is currently no technique that will
certain features   handle this problem.

However, this book includes no guidelines such as this because it concentrates on the cases where some sort of solution, however provisional, is claimed to exist. For this reason, readers should also not read too much into the lack of mention of particular problem features— a problem feature or domain factor might not be mentioned in these guidelines and yet present a stumbling block to an expert-system implementation.

1.4 ORGANIZATION OF DESIGN GUIDELINES

An analysis was made of an earlier version of these design guidelines [Kline and Dolins 1985] to identify general problem features underlying many of the guidelines. Five problem features turned out to be important in this analysis for the proper use of AI implementation techniques [Kline and Dolins 1986]:

1. What kind of connection is there between evidence and hypotheses? There are many kinds of evidence, and different expert-system designs are required to obtain the maximum amount of leverage from each kind.

2. When does the information needed to solve problems become available? Information can be available at program-design time, problem-input time, or problem-solution time.

3. What kind of environment will the expert system operate in? An expert system must be well matched to its operational environment to be useful.

4. How can we help ensure that the expert system will expend its effort wisely? It can be difficult to solve problems within the constraints imposed by computational resources.

5. What counts as a solution, and how many are there likely to be? An expert system is entitled to stop and declare the problem solved under a variety of circumstances.

One chapter of this book is devoted to each of these general problem features. Each chapter describes the general problem feature and provides design guidelines that illustrate that feature. Many of the design guidelines make reference to more than one general problem feature; in such cases the guidelines are described only in the chapter where they best illustrate the general theme.

In addition to the five general problem features identified in Kline and Dolins [1986], there is another general problem feature of importance to expert-system design:

6. What is the nature of the knowledge used to solve problems in this area? Knowledge occurs in a variety of different forms. Depending on the form, different expert-system designs will be appropriate.

Chapter 7 describes the various forms that knowledge can take and provides specific design guidelines for these different forms. There are two main advantages of organizing design guidelines in this way:

1. By having a firm command of these general problem features, knowledge engineers improve their chances of coming up with the right design for expert systems.

2. Awareness of these general problem features should also help knowledge engineers take full advantage of new AI techniques as they emerge.

Descriptions of new AI techniques seldom indicate what features a problem must have in order for that technique to be appropriate. The general problem features provide a set of questions that can be asked about a new technique to determine its appropriate range of application:

1. What does this technique assume about the connection between evidence and hypotheses?
2. What does this new technique assume about the arrival time of information?
3. What kind of operating environment for the expert system would make this technique appropriate?
4. How does this technique affect computational efficiency?
5. What assumptions does this technique make about the nature of solutions?
6. Does this technique assume that a particular kind of knowledge is available or have implications for how the knowledge should be organized?

2 Connecting Evidence to Hypotheses

A wide variety of implementation strategies have been employed in expert systems in order to extract the maximum amount of leverage from evidence. The following guideline is looking for several different kinds of connection between evidence and hypotheses.

2.1 Evidence: Black, White, Gray

Is it possible to construct a test that can be applied to each candidate solution, such that passing the test proves the candidate is a genuine solution? (For example: *A combination is clearly the right one if it opens the safe.*)

or

Is it possible to construct a test, so that failing the test proves the candidate is not a genuine solution? (For example: *Blood tests can rule out paternity, but not establish it.*)

or

Is there only a large "gray area" of better and worse candidates to choose from?

Evidence: Any   Type: Any

Rule candidates in,   → *Generate-and-Test*
and there is an
efficient generator

Rule candidates out   → *Generate-and-Test*, *Pruning*, or *Confirma-*
                            tion by Exclusion

Gray area   → Determine which conclusion has the
                            weight of evidence on its side. Some tech-
                            niques include *Scoring Functions*, *Group-*
                            and-Differentiate, and *Opportunistic Search*.

As this guideline suggests, a test for detecting that a candidate is not
a genuine solution can produce a positive conclusion by eliminating
all but one of a set of candidates, that is, confirmation by exclusion
[Pople 1982, pp. 130f.]. The negative connection between evidence and
hypotheses leads to a different expert-system design than is obtained
when there is total reliance on positive connections.

Guideline 2.6 illustrates a different kind of connection between evidence and hypotheses. A particular piece of evidence can restrict the
solution to a range of possibilities without saying anything about which
possibility is actually the right one—for example, Pople's "constrictors"
[1977, p. 1033]. This kind of connection between evidence and hypotheses leads naturally to expert systems that organize hypotheses into a hierarchy and proceed from general hypotheses such as lung disease to
more specific hypotheses such as emphysema.

Guideline 2.2 indicates that the nature of the connection between evidence and hypotheses influences the choice of "shallow" versus "deep"
reasoning in expert systems. In some diagnosis problems, the evidence
is linked directly to bottom-line conclusions. Shallow reasoning employing heuristic associations is appropriate for these problems. In other diagnosis problems, evidence can be found that also confirms intermediate steps along a causal path connecting ultimate causes to symptoms.
Deep reasoning employing a model of the operative causal relationships may be appropriate for these sorts of problems.

2.1.1 Support for Example Guideline 2.1

Tests for solutions can be effective in several different ways. Some
tests reliably accept solution candidates; others reliably reject solution

candidates. In either case there are reasoning strategies that take maximum advantage of the reliability that is available. Unfortunately, few problems admit a clear-cut distinction between solutions and nonsolutions. A variety of reasoning strategies have been developed to find the "best" available solutions for such problems.

Rule Candidates Out

In many data-analysis tasks it is desirable to find every interpretation that is consistent with the data. This conservative attitude is standard in high-risk applications, such as the analysis of poisonous substances or medical diagnosis. A systematic approach would be to consider all possible cases and to rule out those inconsistent with the data.... The DENDRAL program (Buchanan and Feigenbaum 1978) is probably the best known program that reasons by elimination (using generate-and-test) [p. 149].
— Stefik, M., Aikins, J., Balzer, R., Benoit, J., Birnbaum, L., Hayes-Roth, F., and Sacerdoti, E. The organization of expert systems, a tutorial. *Artificial Intelligence*, *18*, 135–173 (1982). Copyright 1982, Elsevier Science Publishers B.V.

Weight of Evidence

Unfortunately, not every decision can be categorical. No simple rule exists for deciding to perform a bone marrow biopsy or when to discharge a patient from the cardiac intensive care unit. Those decisions must be made by carefully weighing all the evidence.

A number of formal schemes for the weighing of evidence are used, and we shall concentrate on one of them, the *probabilistic* [i.e., Bayes Rule] to contrast with the categorical mode of reasoning[1] [p. 117].
— Szolovits, P., and Pauker, S. G. Categorical and probabilistic reasoning in medical diagnosis. *Artificial Intelligence*, *11*, 115–144 (1978). Copyright 1978, Elsevier Science Publishers B.V.

[1]Other potentially appropriate schemes include the theory of *belief functions* (Shafer, 1976) and the application of *fuzzy set theory* (Gaines, 1976; Zadeh, 1965). All share the characteristic that arithmetic functions are performed to combine separate beliefs or implications to determine their joint effect. We are not convinced of the uniform superiority of any of these formalisms.

2.2 *Visibility of Intermediate Steps*

The following guideline indicates that one of its recommendations, Deep Reasoning, is "expensive." The "expensive" label is a warning that there is much more effort and risk involved in implementing Deep Reasoning than in implementing Shallow Reasoning. Consequently, expert-system designers should be thoroughly convinced that their problem supports the confirmation of intermediate steps before attempting to implement a Deep-Reasoning system. Other design guidelines label some of the recommendations as "cheap," implying easy implementation.

If the expert system will be solving a diagnosis problem, then Can evidence be found that confirms some of the intermediate steps along a causal path connecting ultimate causes to symptoms?

> *or*

Can the intervening causal steps only be determined after we have discovered the correct diagnosis from evidence linking symptoms directly with sets of bottom-line conclusions?

Evidence: Any   Type: Any

Confirm intermediate   → *"Deep" Reasoning*; also called *Causal Mod-*
steps   *els* and *Reasoning from First Principles*
                            {expensive}.

Evidence: Moderate, powerful   Type: Constructed, simulation

Infer intermediate   → *"Shallow" Reasoning*; also called *Heuristic*
steps   *Association* and *Compiled Evidence*—usual-
                          ly implemented with *Rules*.

Type: Preenumerated

Shallow Reasoning

The following two quotes argue that it may be difficult to confirm the occurrence of the events that make up a complete causal description of the system being diagnosed. Shallow-Reasoning systems can avoid having to make reference to causally relevant events that are not readily confirmed.

It turns out that reasoning backwards in terms of a causal model is not always appropriate. As we discovered when explaining the rules, not all of the causal steps of the process can be directly confirmed: we can only assume that they have occurred. For example, rather than providing diagnostic clues, the concept of "portal of entry and passage" is very often deduced from the diagnosis itself.

According to this view, principles are good for summarizing arguments, and good to fall back on when you've lost grasp on the problem, but they don't *drive the process* of medical reasoning. Specifically, (1) if a symptom needs to be explained (is highly unusual), we ask what could cause it ("Strep-viridans? It is normally found in the mouth. How did it get to the heart? Has the patient had dental work recently?"); (2) to "prove" that the diagnosis is correct (after it has been constructed), we use a causal argument ("He has pneumonia; the bacteria obviously got into the blood from the lungs.") Thus causal knowledge can be used to provide feedback that everything fits.

In meningitis diagnosis, the problem is to manage a broad, if not incoherent, hypothesis set, rather than pursue a single causal path. The underlying theory recedes to the background, and the expert tends to approach the problem simply in terms of weak associations between observed data and bottom-line conclusions [pp. 232–233].
  — Clancey, W. J. Extensions to rules for explanation and tutoring. *Artificial Intelligence, 20,* 215–251 (1983). Copyright 1983, Elsevier Science Publishers B.V.

Shallow-reasoning systems are called "evidentially oriented systems" in the following quote and Deep-Reasoning systems are called "model-driven."

Presumably, the most generally applicable causal descriptions are those stated in terms of the fundamental laws of physics. Attempts to describe phenomena at this level, however, are generally impractical, not only for expert systems, but for many sciences as well. The objects of concern to biologists, psychologists, and, of course, engineers, are at a much higher level of description. So the issue is then one of picking a level of description that is appropriate to the task at hand. How can this level be characterized for an expert diagnostic task?

I think the following two constraints on a level of description are reasonable.

• The level of description should be deep enough to depict events or states, the occurrence of which must be recognized for a model driven diagnostic system to be successful (or diagnostically competent).

- It must be possible for either the system or the user to recognize events under these descriptions as necessary to drive diagnoses.

If we use these criteria to determine the kind of knowledge MUD would have needed, if designed as a causally oriented system, we can see two things. The first is that there is a tremendous scope to the kind of knowledge that is required to model relevant events. The second is that as the level of description is pushed deeper to become more general, and diagnostically competent, it is likely that neither the system nor the user would be able to recognize events under these descriptions at run time.

It appeared that a prohibitive amount of development time would be required to achieve a model driven diagnostic system in the mud domain [that is, oil-well drilling fluids]. There are just too many different kinds of considerations. Secondly, in any particular run time context, it appeared that there would be too many free parameters to allow a model to efficiently achieve a unique termination condition of diagnostic significance.

But why is an evidentially oriented system immune to (or less subject to) difficulties in a domain affected by many different kinds of considerations? The main reason is that such systems can abstract over incomplete knowledge. For instance, MUD's compiled representation assigns a small negative weight to the salt contamination hypothesis when there is no evidence that there is an increase in the yield point. The reason for this is that a mud engineer will not definitely reject this hypothesis on this particular lack of evidence, because there may be many reasons for not observing it in a particular case. The system need not know or be able to determine exactly why an increase in yield point is not observed; and yet a reasonable diagnosis can be achieved. Of course, if knowledge of these exception conditions were accessible and compiled into MUD's knowledge base, it could assign a high negative weight when none [of these exception conditions] held. The point, however, is that an evidential system can prove effective when this additional knowledge hasn't been or can't be built in. This is generally not true with a dynamic model [pp. 25f.].
> — Kahn, G. On when diagnostic systems want to do without causal knowledge. In *ECAI-84: Advances in Artificial Intelligence*, T. O'Shea (ed.), Elsevier, 1984, pp. 21–30. Copyright 1984, Elsevier Science Publishers B.V.

2.3 Generalized Evidence

The following guideline discusses some of the circumstances that argue against linking symptoms directly to bottom-line conclusions.

Will the expert system be solving a diagnosis problem?

and

Is it important to accurately assess causal relationships in this domain so that predisposing factors are recognized as such and treated differently from findings actually caused by the underlying condition?

or

Do the findings observed depend strongly on the severity of the underlying condition or the degree of its progression?

or

Are there sets of correlated findings that tend to occur together under several different diagnostic outcomes?

Evidence: Any   Type: Any

Yes, to any of these   → *Intermediate Hypotheses*

Errors in INTERNIST-1's diagnoses led its developers to break up exhaustive lists of disease manifestations into sets that correspond to a sequence of states. Predisposing factors make up a separate state, as do manifestations that frequently occur simultaneously. Manifestations associated with severe or advanced cases of a disease are associated with states that occur later in the sequence.

> A diagnostic program must be able to recognize the appropriate cause or causes of observed findings in a patient. A justification for each diagnosis must be developed on a pathophysiologic or causal framework that is consistent with established medical knowledge. To its detriment, INTERNIST-1's handling of explanation is shallow. When the program concludes a diagnosis, that diagnosis is allowed to explain any observed manifestations that are listed on its disease profile. Once explained, a manifestation is no longer used to evoke new disease hypotheses or to participate in the scoring process. This situation is compounded by the inadequate representation of causality in the INTERNIST-1 knowledge base. Disease profiles contain, in an undifferentiated manner, factors predisposing to the illness as well as findings that result from the disease process itself.

What is required is a restructuring of the knowledge base to include intermediate-level pathophysiologic states and the segregation of predisposing factors from findings actually caused by the disease. Diseases should be profiled in terms of their intermediate states, rather than as exhaustive lists of manifestations. If the program had such a feature, the presence or absence of each state would be independently determined, and a disease would be allowed to explain a finding only when the state causing that finding had been confirmed.

A related problem not handled well by INTERNIST–1 is the interdependency of manifestations. For example, persons with elevated conjugated bilirubin levels in their blood usually have bilirubinuria. At present the evoking strengths of each finding count redundantly toward any diagnosis that can explain them. This phenomenon causes INTERNIST–1 to favor disproportionately the most common explanation for a set of findings. A solution would be the creation of an intermediate state, "abnormal bilirubin metabolism and transport," which would explain both conjugated hyperbilirubinemia and bilirubinuria. Appropriate weight for the intermediate state (rather than for the interdependent manifestations) could be given to any diseases that cause it. Thus creation of a causal network of pathophysiologic states, interposed between observable manifestations and final diagnoses, would allow a diagnostic program to attribute findings to causes accurately and would help to diminish the influence of interdependent manifestations of disease [p. 474].

   — Miller, R. A., Pople, H. E., Jr., and Myers, J. D. INTERNIST-1, an experimental computer-based diagnostic consultant for general internal medicine, *New England Journal of Medicine*, 307, 468–476 (1982). Copyright 1982, Massachusetts Medical Society.

2.4 Confirmation by Exclusion

Is clinching evidence in support of conclusions sometimes unavailable?

and

In these cases is it possible to be confident that the correct conclusion is one of a small number of possibilities?

and

Is clinching evidence available against some of the possibilities?

                Evidence: Moderate, powerful   Type: Any

Yes → *Confirmation by Exclusion*

Thus, provided an appropriate differential diagnosis set has been identified, it is possible for the program to come to the correct diagnosis by ruling out all but one of the diagnoses in the set, then recording the remaining contender as its default judgment. In this fashion the program often manages to solve difficult clinical problems even in the absence of clinching data (obtainable only by biopsy or autopsy, perhaps) that are unavailable at the time of the workup [Pople 1982, p. 149].

> — Pople, H. E., Jr. Heuristic methods for imposing structure on ill-structured problems: The structuring of medical diagnostics. In *Artificial Intelligence in Medicine*, P. Szolovits (ed). Boulder, CO: Westview Press, American Association for the Advancement of Science, 1982, pp. 119–190. Copyright 1982, American Association for the Advancement of Science. Reprinted by permission.

2.5 Levels of Detail

Does solving a problem in this domain require a chain of reasoning involving subdomains that are understood in quite different degrees of detail?

or

Is there great variability in the amount of detail that is provided by different pieces of evidence?

Evidence: Any   Type: Constructed, simulation

Yes, subdomains of   → Break the knowledge base into several dif-
different detail or   ferent *Levels of Description* and describe
evidence of variable   the relations between the levels {expen-
detail   sive}.

Medical knowledge about different diseases and their pathophysiology is understood in varying degrees of detail. While it may be easier for a program to reason succinctly with medical knowledge artificially represented at a uniform level of detail, we must be able to reason with medical knowledge at different levels of detail to exploit all of the medical knowledge available. Although this does not pose any difficulty in medical domains where the pathophysiology of diseases is not well developed, in a domain such as electrolyte and acid-base disturbances where, on the one hand, the pathophysiology of the disturbances is well developed and, on the other, the pathophysiology of many of the diseases leading to these disturbances is relatively poorly understood, we are constantly faced with this problem.

Secondly, the information about a patient parallels the physician's medical knowledge about diseases and therefore also comes at different levels of detail. For example, "serum creatine concentration of 1.5" is at a distinctly different level than "high serum creatine," and "lower gastrointestinal loss" than "diarrhea." We need some mechanism by which we can interrelate these concepts. Finally, to be effective in diagnostic problem solving and communicating with clinicians, we ought to have the ability to portray the diagnostic problem in a small and compact space. Yet to be efficacious, we must maintain the ability to take every possible detail into consideration. We have solved this problem by representing the medical knowledge in five distinct levels of detail from a deep pathophysiological level to a more aggregate level of clinical knowledge about disease associations [p. 894].

— Patil, R. S., Szolovits, P., and Schwartz, W. B. Causal understanding of patient illness in medical diagnosis. *Proceedings of the Seventh International Joint Conference on Artificial Intelligence*, 1981, pp. 893–899. Used by permission of the International Joint Conferences on Artificial Intelligence, Inc.; copies of this and other IJCAI Proceedings are available from Morgan Kaufmann Publishers, Inc., PO Box 50490, Palo Alto, CA 94303, USA.

2.6 *Generalized Hypotheses*

Is it frequently the case that a particular piece of evidence restricts the solution to a range of possibilities without saying much about which of those possibilities is actually the right one?

Evidence: Any   Type: Preenumerated

Yes → Associate manifestations with sets of possible conclusions; these sets usually take the form of a stored *Hierarchy of Hypotheses*. The amount of support received by various sets of possible conclusions can be calculated with *Dempster–Shafer Uncertainty Management* or *Bayes Nets* [Pearl 1988, pp. 333–344].

No → Associate manifestations with individual conclusions.

If the focus of attention is directed at higher levels of the disease hierarchy rather than at the terminal level nodes, quite specific associations between very commonplace manifestations and these higher level disease descriptors can often be established. For example—jaundice, which is a readily observed physical sign, is a reasonably strong cue that some problem within the general category of liver disease is present, although it provides virtually no help in further discrimination within this subarea. Similarly, bloody sputum, while not pathognomonic with respect to any particular lung problem, provides ample justification for serious consideration of the lung area as a problem focus.

The existence of these specific patterns of association between certain commonly observed manifestations and higher-level disease descriptors has led to the conjecture that the clinician's facility in delineating the multi-problem structure of a clinical case derives, at least in part, from his attentions to what we have called the "constrictors" of a case—those findings that strongly cue the hypothesizing of some unspecified problem within each of several categories of the disease hierarchy.

Because constrictors come with varying degrees of certitude, it is important to recognize the heuristic nature of any multi-problem formation strategy based on this concept. Hence, it is still necessary to view the problem-formation process as conjectural, and have provision for retreating from any multi-problem hypothesis that might be adduced, in order to consider other alternatives [p. 1033].
> — Pople, H. E., Jr. The formation of composite hypotheses in diagnostic problem solving: An exercise in synthetic reasoning. *Proceedings of the Fifth International Joint Conference on Artificial Intelligence*, Cambridge, MA, 1977, pp. 1030–1037. Used by permission of the International Joint Conferences on Artificial Intelligence, Inc.; copies of this and other IJCAI Proceedings are available from Morgan Kaufmann Publishers, Inc., PO Box 50490, Palo Alto, CA 94303, USA.

What attracted us to the D-S (Dempster–Shafer) theory, however, and left us dissatisfied with the approach to singleton hypotheses proposed by Barnett, is the [Dempster–Shafer] theory's potential for handling evidence bearing on categories of diseases as well as on specific disease entities. We are unaware of another model that suggests how evidence concerning hierarchically-related hypotheses might be combined coherently and consistently to allow inexact reasoning at whatever level of abstraction is appropriate for the evidence gathered at varying levels of detail or specificity. Much of our frustration with the original MYCIN representation scheme and the CF model resulted from their inability to handle such hierarchical relationships cleanly.

In actual practice, decisions about treatment are often made on the basis of high-level categories rather than specific organism identities (e.g., "I'm quite sure that this is one of the enterics (i.e., the Enterobacteriaceae), and would therefore treat with an aminoglycoside and a cephalosporin (i.e., two types of antibiotic), but I have no idea which of the enteric organisms is causing the disease.").

Problems such as this would be better handled if experts could specify rules which refer to semantic concepts at whatever level in the domain hierarchy is most natural and appropriate. They should ideally not be limited to the most specific level—the singleton hypotheses in the frame of discernment—but should be free to use more unifying concepts [pp. 343f.].

> — Gordon, J., and Shortliffe, E. H. A method for managing evidential reasoning in a hierarchical hypothesis space. *Artificial Intelligence*, *26*, 323–357 (1985). Copyright 1985, Elsevier Science Publishers B.V.

2.7 Levels of Abstraction

Does solving the problem involve transformations between several different levels of description?

or

Are several diverse knowledge sources available?

Evidence: Any   Type: Constructed, simulation

Yes → Use a *Blackboard* data structure to record hypotheses.

The first quote describes the use of Blackboards in the HEARSAY-II speech understanding system. The "diversity of transformations" mentioned in the quote is a reference to the different levels of linguistic description that are commonly distinguished. HEARSAY-II distinguised between the following levels in describing speech inputs: segment, syllable, word, word sequence, and phrase. The second quote describes the use of Blackboards in the HASP/SIAP expert system.

The necessity for diverse KSs [Knowledge Sources] derives from the diversity of transformations used by the speaker in creating the acoustic signal and the corresponding inverse transformations needed by the listener for interpreting it.... Because each KS is an *independent* condition-

action module, KSs communicate through a global database called the *blackboard* [Erman, Hayes-Roth, Lesser, and Reddy 1980, p. 218].
— Copyright 1980, Association for Computing Machinery, Inc. Reprinted by permission.

It was the idea of fusing uncertain and partial solutions to construct solutions, combined with "island-driving,"[2] that intrigued the designers.

The sonar analysts solved the problem piecemeal. They first identified a harmonic set in the signals. The "accounted-for" signals were then "subtracted" from the data set. Then another harmonic set would be formed with the remaining data, and so on until all the signals were accounted for.[3] Each harmonic set implied a set of possible sources of sound (for example, a propellar shaft), which in turn implied a set of possible ship types from which the sounds could be emanating. Certain signal characteristics directly implied platform types, but this type of diversion from the incremental analysis was very rare. What the human analysts were doing was what might be called logical induction and synthesis.[4] Hypotheses were synthesized from pieces of data using a large amount of domain-specific knowledge that translated information in one form to information in another form, that is, transformed a description in one vocabulary to one in another vocabulary. For example, a set of frequencies was transformed into a set of possible ship parts (for example, a shaft or a propellar) by using knowledge of the form, "If the harmonic set consists of..., then it is likely to...." The partial solutions thus formed were then combined using other knowledge to construct acceptable solutions.

Once it was clear that interpretation in HASP, as in HEARSAY, was a process of piecemeal generation of partial solutions that were combined to form complete solutions, the HEARSAY-II system organization could be exploited. The CBH [Current Best Hypothesis] was partitioned into levels of analysis corresponding to the way analysts were used to thinking (that is, signals, harmonic sets, sources, and ship types). The rule-based knowledge gathered for the purposes of pruning and guiding the search

---

[2]*Island driving* is a problem solving strategy. A relatively reliable partial hypothesis is designated as an "island of certainty," and the hypothesis building pushes out from this solution island in many directions. This is sometimes called a "Middle-out" strategy. There can be many islands of certainty driving the problem-solving process.

[3]As easy as it sounds, the task of harmonic set formation was a very difficult one, given noisy and missing data, and could produce large combinatorial possibilities. Addressing this problem became one of the major concerns in HASP.

[4]An interesting article on this point is "A more rational view of logic," by Alex P. Pentland and Martin Fischler; it appeared in the Winter, 1983 issue of the *AI Magazine*.

process was organized into sets of rules (knowledge sources) that transformed information on one level to information on another level.[5] [Nii 1986].

    — Reprinted with permission from *AI Magazine*, 1986, pp. 50f., published by the American Association for Artificial Intelligence.

2.8   Single Focus or Multiple Possibilities

Do experts typically make an initial guess at one solution, which they then go on to confirm or disconfirm?

   or

Do they generate several candidate hypotheses and then discriminate between them?

         Evidence: Weak, moderate   Type: Preenumerated, constructed

Initial guess at one   → *Model-Driven Reasoning*, which is also
solution   called *Expectation-Driven Reasoning*.

Several hypotheses   → *Group-and-Differentiate*

Expectation-Driven Reasoning

The following quote describes problem characteristics that support a recommendation of Model-Driven Reasoning. Care must be taken to differentiate between making a single hypothesis be the focus of the reasoning and making a set of hypotheses be the focus of the reasoning, as these have different implications for implementation techniques.

The characteristics of the PUFF problem that make it a good application for an expectation-driven control strategy include:

1. A large amount of input data.

---

[5]It is interesting to note that many of the pieces of knowledge intended for pruning purposes could be converted into inductive knowledge. For example, a pruning rule that read "If a signal is coming from outside the normal traffic lane, then its source could not be cargo or cruise ships" could be used directly for reducing alternatives or could be converted to read "..., then its source is either military ships or fishing boats." One can hold the view that this is not surprising, because knowledge is knowledge, and what counts is how and when it's used.

2. A small solution space.

3. A simple model for initial hypotheses [Aiello 1983, p. 4].

Group-and-Differentiate

In the following quote, the "Precaution" method describes a Group-and-Differentiate strategy, whereas the "Extraction" method appears to pursue a single hypothesis initially with a fall back to a set of hypotheses on failure of the initial hypotheses. Extraction thus appears to be a mixture of Expectation-Driven Reasoning and the Group-and-Differentiate strategy.

> For the two high-level experts in the study [of pediatric cardiology cases], two distinct methods of using the LCS [logical competitor set] were also identified:
>
> 1. *Precaution.* This involves the generation and use *together* as hypotheses of the full set of logical competitors, enabling them to be weighed against each other and the data.
> 2. *Extraction.* This method involves more aggressive focus on a member of the set, with full expansion to the remainder of the set as disconfirmatory evidence for the target member is found.
>
> Medical students, after six weeks of training and clinical practice in the field represented by the cases, generally showed neither expert form nor expert substance. Students hardly ever considered the full LCS and focused on the "classic" members in cases that encouraged this [Feltovich, Johnson, Moller, and Swanson 1984, p. 311].

2.9 Crucial Step in Search

Is it possible to conclude at program-design time that a certain crucial step will be required to solve the problem? (One way to tell that a step is crucial is to ask if you are willing to temporarily increase the distance to your final goal in order to achieve that step.)

                    Evidence: Moderate, powerful   Type: Constructed

Yes → *Means-Ends Analysis*

Means-Ends Analysis is the search strategy employed in the General Problem-Solver (GPS) system. The MOLGEN system, which designs genetics experiments [Stefik 1981a,b], is an example of an expert system that uses Means-Ends Analysis.

> In many state-space search problems it is not too difficult to guess the identity of at least one of the state-space operators that will occur somewhere in the solution sequence of operators. That is, although the problem of specifying the entire sequence of operators is difficult, the problem of specifying one of them is often easy. The possibility of finding one such operator is enhanced when the problem is such that the application of one of the operators is regarded as a crucial step in the problem solution. (In terms of the state-space graph, the application of such an operator corresponds to an arc linking otherwise almost separate parts of the graph.) For example, in the Tower of Hanoi problem...the operator "Move disk C to peg 3" can be singled out as a crucial step in the problem solution [p. 104].

> The notion of key operators and differences and their use in problem solving is due largely to Newell and his coworkers on GPS [see Ernst and Newell (1969)] [pp. 112–113] [Nilsson 1971].
>   — *Problem Solving Methods in Artificial Intelligence*, © 1971 by McGraw-Hill. Reprinted by permission.

3 The Arrival Time of Information

It takes information to solve problems, and an adequate solution cannot be found until all the relevant information has been assembled. Various pieces of the information used to solve problems can become available at program-design time, data-input time, or problem-solution time. If the necessary information or knowledge is available at program-design time, then it is generally possible to build that knowledge directly into the design of an expert system. In other cases, important information becomes available only at problem-input time or after some progress has been made toward finding a solution (i.e., problem-solution time). In these cases, a design must be found to take advantage of the information as it becomes available.

Knowledge engineers should appreciate that whenever they identify a crucial item of information that makes it possible to solve problems in a domain, they also need to establish the expected arrival time of that information. For example, Guideline 3.1 determines whether constraint propagation techniques will be required to find the values of variables. If it is known at *program-design time* that the values of certain variables will always be provided as part of a problem description, then forward-chaining can be used to determine the values of the other variables. However, if it is necessary to wait until *data-input time* to discover which variables have known values, then more general constraint propagation techniques will have to be employed. The choice between Forward-Chaining and Constraint Propagation depends on exactly when it will become clear which variables will be the first to receive values.

3.1 Constraint Propagation or Forward-Chaining

Is it necessary to find values for a number of variables where the variables can take on numeric or Boolean (i.e., true or false) values?

and

Are there constraints among the variables that make it possible to use the known values of some of the variables to solve for other variables?

and

Does the identity of the variables whose values are known at data-input time differ from problem to problem?

Evidence: Any   Type: Any

Yes, differ from problem to problem	→ *Constraint Propagation*
No, same variables known at outset	→ *Forward-Chaining Rules*

Other implementation strategies for expert systems are appropriate when certain kinds of information are available at program-design time. For example, Guideline 3.2 asks whether it is possible at program-design time to anticipate the major areas of uncertainty and unreliability the expert system will face. If so, then building redundancy into the design will help deal with the uncertainty.

Besides program-design time and problem-input time, there are cases in which crucial information does not appear until a partial solution to a problem has been obtained. As described in Guideline 3.3, opportunistic search strategies wait for "islands" of certainty to emerge and then use those islands to help interpret neighboring regions of greater uncertainty. Although the islands of certainty are crucial to solving a problem, it is impossible to say where those islands will be found until a certain amount of progress has been made toward developing a solution.

3.1.1 Support for Example Guideline 3.1

The following quote contrasts the use of rules "when device behavior is uncomplicated" with the use of constraints. A complicating feature of the discussion is that constraints are generally implemented *using* rules, and, as a result, the distinction between rules and constraints threatens to disappear. However, there is a clear difference in philosophy that should not be lost sight of. In the case where the same variables are known at the outset of each problem, then the simplest thing to do is write rules that describe how these known values can be used to infer the values of unknown variables.

As illustrated in the quote, however, it is possible to model an adder by writing a set of rules that encode all possible ways of inferring unknown variables from known variables. In a case such as this, the rules are used only to implement the simple algebraic constraint *input-1 + input-2 = sum*, and it is possible to imagine other implementations of that constraint that don't rely on rules at all.

> A variety of techniques have been used to describe behavior, including simple rules for mapping inputs to outputs, Petri nets, and unrestricted chunks of code. Simple rules are useful when device behavior is uncomplicated; Petri nets are useful when the focus is on modeling parallel events; and unrestricted code is often the last resort when more structured forms of expression prove too limited or awkward. Various combinations of these techniques have also been explored.

> Our initial implementation is based on the use of constraints [Sussman and Steele 1980]. Conceptually a constraint is simply a relationship. The behavior of the adder,...,for example, can be expressed by saying that the logic levels of the terminals on ports *input-1, input-2,* and *sum* have an obvious relationship.

> In practice, this relationship is implemented by defining a set of rules covering all different computations (the three for the adder are shown below) and setting them up as demons that watch the appropriate terminals. (A demon is a chunk of code that can be run asynchronously: it is fired whenever all its input becomes available.) A complete description of a module, then, is composed of its structural description as outlined

earlier and a behavioral description in the form of rules that interrelate the logic levels at its terminals.

- to get sum from input-1 and input-2 do (+ input-1 input-2)
- to get input-1 from sum and input-2 do (− sum input-2)
- to get input-2 from sum and input-1 do (− sum input-1)

A set of rules like these is in keeping with the original conception of constraints, which emphasized the nondirectional relationship character of the information. When we attempt to use it to model causality and function, however, we have to be careful. This approach is well-suited to modeling causality and behavior of analog circuits, since these devices are largely nondirectional. But we can hardly say that the last two rules are a good description of the *behavior* of an adder chip—the device doesn't do subtraction; putting logic levels at its output and one input does not cause a logic level to appear on its other input.

The last two rules really model the inferences we make about the device. Hence our implementation distinguishes between simulation rules that represent *flow of electricity* (digital behavior, the first rule) and rules representing *flow of inference* (conclusions we can make about the device, the next two rules) [Davis and Shrobe 1983, p. 78].
— © 1983 by IEEE. Reprinted by permission.

3.2 Anticipate–Assess–Resolve Uncertainty

Can we anticipate the major areas of uncertainty and unreliability ahead of time when we design the expert system?

or

Is it important to accurately assess the amount of uncertainty to be attached to the expert system's conclusion for a particular problem?

or

Will the expert system need to take active measures to reduce or discount the particular uncertainties encountered when working on a problem?

Evidence: Weak, moderate   Type: Any

Anticipate uncertainty → Build in *Redundancy* in those areas where uncertainty is anticipated.

Assess amount of uncertainty	→ Numerical *Scoring Functions* such as *Bayes Rule*, *Dempster–Shafer*, *Fuzzy-Set Theory*, or *EMYCIN Certainty Factors*.
Resolve uncertainty	→ *Reason Explicitly about Uncertainty*. For example, have rules that decide what evidence should be believed, or keep track of the reasons for believing or disbelieving hypotheses and choose tasks according to the type of uncertainties they can resolve (e.g., *Endorsement-Based Approaches to Uncertainty*).

These alternatives are not mutually exclusive. However, as the following quote points out, there is some degree of incompatibility between redundancy and a completely accurate assessment of uncertainty. This is because redundancy will often produce violations of the independence assumptions that are typically invoked to demonstrate the soundness of a scoring function.

Redundancy

The best answer we have found for dealing with uncertainty is redundancy. By that we mean using multiple, overlapping sources of knowledge to reach conclusions, and using the overlap as checks and balances on the correctness of the contributions made by different knowledge sources. In MYCIN we try to exploit the overlaps in the information contributed by laboratory and clinical data, just as physicians must. For example, a high fever and a high white blood cell count both provide information about the severity of an infection. On the assumption that the correct data will point more coherently to the correct conclusions than the incorrect data will, we expect the erroneous data to have very little effect after all the evidence has been gathered. The *absence* of a few data points will also have little overall effect if other, overlapping evidence has been found. Overlapping inference paths, or redundancy in the rules, also helps correct problems of a few incorrect or missing inferences. With several lines of reasoning leading from data to conclusions, a few can be wrong (and a few can be missing), and the system still ends up with correct conclusions.

We recognize that introducing redundant data and inference rules is at odds with the independence assumption of the CF [EMYCIN Certainty

Factor] model. We did not want the system to fail for want of one or two items of information. When we encounter cases with missing evidence, a redundant reasoning path ensures the robustness of the system. In cases where the overlapping pieces of evidence are all present, however, nothing inside the system prevents it from using the dependent information multiple times. We thus have to correct for this in the rule set itself. The dependencies may be syntactic—for example, use of the same concept in several rules—in which case an intelligent editor can help detect them. Or they may be semantic—for example, use of causally related concepts—in which case physicians writing or reviewing the rules have to catch them [Buchanan and Shortliffe 1984, pp. 684f.].

— Buchanan/Shortliffe, *Rule-Based Expert Systems*, © 1984 by B. G. Buchanan and E. H. Shortliffe. Reprinted with permission of Addison-Wesley Publishing Co., Inc., Reading, Massachusetts.

Kahn and McDermott [1984] argue that by relying on redundancy they can ignore the fact that some of their data are unreliable in the drilling fluids domain.

The current version of MUD assumes that all data entered, as well as the recognition of diagnostically significant observations, is certain. So far, surprisingly, this has not degraded MUD's performance. We had expected that MUD would need a way of both recognizing the likelihood of a deviation in a mud property and of transmitting evidential uncertainty to its hypothetical conclusions. In fact, MUD is designed to allow this functionality if it becomes desirable.

MUD seems able to succeed with its assumption that its data is certain because its diagnostic procedure is robust in two respects. First, there are typically several diagnostically significant observations that can evoke a hypothesis; if a problem occurs it is likely to be indicated by forcing at least one mud property across a detection threshold. Thus, uncertainty in the data is unlikely to cause MUD to miss the occurrence of a disruptive event. Secondly, as MUD brings several evidential considerations together in coming to a conclusion with respect to any hypothesis, small errors in some fractions of these observations may wash out given a preponderance of evidence for or against the hypothesis.[1] Indeed, this might explain why mud engineers themselves do not need to rely on mathematical models for handling uncertainty [Kahn and McDermott 1984, p. 121].

— © 1984 by IEEE. Reprinted by permission.

---

[1] One place where it is necessary to be careful is when a mud property with a high negative-support value is near a detection threshold. In these cases, MUD warns the user, but does not alter its diagnostic conclusion since the detection threshold, set by the engineer, should take into account the desirable tradeoff between false-positive and false-negative responses. If the latter is of concern, the threshold can be lowered; if the former, the threshold can be raised.

Reason Explicitly about Certainty and Use Redundancy

Although the MYCIN certainty factor mechanism [Shortliffe and Buchanan 1975] is incorporated into the VM (Ventilator Manager) structure, it has not been used. Most of the representation of uncertainty has been encoded symbolically in the contents of each rule. Rules conclude that measurement values can be spurious (under specified conditions), and the interpreter prohibits using such aberrant values for further inferences. Any value associated with a measured parameter that was concluded too long ago is considered to be unknown and, therefore, no longer useful in the reasoning mechanism. This is meant to be a first approximation to our intuition that confidence in an interpretation decays over time unless it is reinforced by new observations.

Uncertainty has been implicitly incorporated in the VM knowledge base in the formulation of some rules. In order to make conclusions with a higher level of certainty, premise clauses were added to rules that correlated strongly with existing premise clauses—e.g., using both mean and systolic blood pressures. The choice of measurement ranges in several therapy rules also took into account the element of uncertainty. Although the experts wanted four or five parameters within the IDEAL limit prior to suggesting the transition to the next optimal therapy state, they often used the ACCEPTABLE limits. In fact, it would be unlikely that all measurements would simultaneously fall into IDEAL range. Therefore, incorporating these "grey areas" into the definition of the symbolic ranges was appropriate. There are at least two possible explanations for the lack of certainty factors in [the] VM rule base: (1) on the wards, it is only worthwhile to make an inference if one strongly believes and can support the conclusion; and (2) the measurements available from the monitoring system were chosen because of their high correlation with patients' conditions.

The PUFF [Aikins, Kunz, Shortliffe, and Fallat 1983] and SACON [Bennett and Engelmore 1981] systems also did not use the certainty factor mechanism. The main goal of these systems was to classify or categorize a small number of conclusions as opposed to making fine distinctions between competing hypotheses [Fagan, Kunz, Feigenbaum and Osborn 1984, pp. 416–417]

> — Buchanan/Shortliffe, *Rule-Based Expert Systems*, © 1984 by B. G. Buchanan and E. H. Shortliffe. Reprinted with permission of Addison-Wesley Publishing Co., Inc., Reading, Massachusetts.

Assess Amount of Uncertainty or Resolve Uncertainty

The following quote contrasts numerical approaches to uncertainty assessment with endorsement-based approaches to uncertainty. In another part of his thesis [p. 168] Paul Cohen makes it clear that there is no necessary incompatibility between an endorsement-based approach and numerical approaches.

> Some aspects of the endorsement-based approach are cumbersome compared with the elegant numerical approaches, but endorsements have one major advantage over numbers: They contain *explicit* information about why one believes and disbelieves. Consequently, one can *reflect* on these records to decide how to act. The previous section outlined half a dozen resolutions that might apply to a conflict of values, such as averaging, hedging, worst-case analysis, and ignoring the discrepancy. It is obvious that these methods are not equally applicable to all kinds of conflicts, and just as obvious that one cannot choose an applicable method based on the degrees of belief of the conflicting hypotheses. An explicit record of the *kind* of conflict is needed.
>
> These considerations suggest that the endorsement-based approach might be inappropriate for domains in which numerical degrees of belief have a clear semantics and are adequate representations of all of the information about uncertainty that one might want to express, simply because the calculus of Bayesian inference or belief functions is very much less cumbersome than that of the model of endorsement. If we are satisfied that all degrees of belief have a common interpretation, such as a mixture of utility and probability arguments; and/or we do not care to separate these conceptual components of degrees of belief; and we are satisfied that our representation of uncertainty has the passive role of measuring how much we believe, instead of an active part in reducing, or at least discounting, uncertainty; and we do not need explanations of why we believe and disbelieve hypotheses; then the numerical approach to uncertainty might be preferable. Moreover, if we demand a normative calculus to ensure rational decisions, then we will prefer some numerical methods to the model of endorsement, at least for the process of assessment and combining of evidence. On the other hand, if we think that numerical degrees of belief mask distinctions that could be profitably used to reason about uncertainty, if we wish to regard kinds of uncertainty as problems to be solved by resolution or discounting methods, if we doubt that the requirements of normative approaches are met, and acknowledge that numerical methods are at best heuristic anyway, then the model of endorsement stands as an interesting and potentially powerful tool.
>
> Much of the power of the model of endorsement derives from recognizing different kinds of uncertainty and resolving them in appropriate ways [Cohen 1983, pp. 169f.].
> — Reprinted by permission of author.

3.3 Island-Driving

Will the expert system be solving a data-interpretation problem?

and

Is it possible to systematically consider the set of possible solutions or solution fragments and evaluate each of them for their compatibility with the data?

or

Will it be necessary to look for parts of the data whose interpretation is unambiguous, and having found them, use them to guide the interpretation of adjacent regions where there is more ambiguity?

Evidence: Any   Type: Constructed

Systematically   → *Generate-and-Test*
evaluate candidates

Unambiguous first   → *Opportunistic Search*

Generate-and-Test

> Heuristic DENDRAL is organized as a Plan–Generate–Test sequence. This is not necessarily the same method used by chemists, but is easily understood by them. It complements their methods by providing such a meticulous search through the space of molecular structures that the chemist is virtually guaranteed that any candidate structure which fails to appear on the final list of plausible structures has been rejected for explicitly stated chemical reasons [Buchanan and Feigenbaum 1978, p. 314].

Opportunistic Search

The following two quotes contrast Opportunistic Search with Generate-and-Test. The references to a "uniform generator of hypotheses" and a "legal move generator" are talking about the generator that allows the Generate-and-Test method to systematically search the space of candidate solutions.

> *Opportunistic search* buys us the benefits of the search model without the necessity of defining a single uniform generator of hypotheses within

the space. The method takes advantage of a scientist's knowledge about what to do next: how to construct a partial explanation of data and how to modify and refine it into a satisfactory, more complete explanation. In problem areas for which a generator of the entire space cannot be defined, or implemented efficiently, a collection of opportunistic rules can provide a method for finding plausible explanations. They start with small "islands of certainty," that is, interpretations of parts of the data that are nearly unambiguous. Then the rules augment the best hypothesis, postulate alternatives to try to disconfirm and note the expected data that would confirm or disconfirm an hypothesis. Since hypothesis elements are considered because there is some positive reason to do so, the exploration is focused on the relevant parts of the space [Buchanan 1983, p. 143].
— *PSA 1982*, Volume 2. Copyright 1983. Reprinted by permission of the Philosophy of Science Association.

Building a signal interpretation system within the program organization described above can best be described as *opportunistic* analysis. Bits and pieces of information must be used as opportunity arises to build slowly a coherent picture of the world—much like putting a jigsaw puzzle together. Some thoughts on the characteristics of problems suited to this approach are listed below.

1. *Large amounts of signal data need to be analyzed.* Examples include the interpretation of speech and other acoustic signals, x-ray and other spectral data, radar signals, photographic data, etc. A variation involves understanding a large volume of symbolic data; for example, the maintenance of a global plotboard of air traffic based on messages from various air traffic control centers.

2. *Formal or informal interpretive theories exist.* By informal interpretive theory we mean *lore* or heuristics which human experts bring to bear in order to *understand* the data. These inexact and informal rules are incorporated as KSs [Knowledge Sources] in conjunction with more formal knowledge about the domain.

3. *Task domain can be decomposed hierarchically in a natural way.* In many cases the domain can be decomposed into a series of data reduction levels, where various interpretive theories (in the sense described above) exist for transforming data from one level to another.

4. *"Opportunistic" strategies must be used.* That is, there is no computationally feasible *legal move generator* that defines the space of solutions in which pruning and steering take place. Rather, by reasoning about bits and pieces of available evidence, one can incrementally generate partial hypotheses that will eventually lead to a more global solution hypothesis.

[Nii, Feigenbaum, Anton, and Rockmore 1982].
— Reprinted with permission from *AI Magazine*, 1982, pp. 34–35, published
by the American Association for Artificial Intelligence.

3.4 Extent of Planning Prior to Execution

Is this a planning problem?

and

**Is the environment predictable enough that the information needed
to form a complete plan is available prior to the execution of any of
those steps?**

or

**Does the information needed to effectively plan later steps only be-
come available following the execution of earlier steps?**

Evidence: Any   Type: Constructed

Available prior to execution	→ Plan entire solution, then execute. *Replanning* remaining steps may be required if events do not go as expected.
Available following execution	→ *Reactive Planning*

For many domains, particularly those created artificially as in a laboratory or on a factory floor, it makes sense to construct a detailed plan
well in advance of execution because the situations expected can be anticipated and controlled. However, it is becoming clear that in more dynamic worlds, where agents exist whose actions cannot be anticipated,
the situation at execution time cannot be controlled, and detailed plans
cannot be built in advance. As one would expect, the solution to this difficulty is to leave some, most, or even all of the planning to take place
during execution when the situation can be determined directly. Systems
that build or change their plans in response to the shifting situations at
execution time are called reactive planners.

The choice of which detailed actions to put in a plan usually depends on
the context in which they will be executed. If that context cannot be computed in advance then the actions cannot be chosen appropriately. For

example, planning the arm motions for the loading portions of a delivery task is both pointless and impossible before the cargo and the loading docks have been examined. More generally, having to choose actions at execution time is unavoidable in any domain where there is uncertainty about what will be encountered after an action is executed. Such uncertainty arises when independent agents or processes can change the world, when actions might not work exactly right, or when there are just too many interacting variables involved in predicting the future [Firby 1987].
    — Reprinted with permission from *Proceedings of the National Conference on Artificial Intelligence (AAAI-87)*, 1987, p. 202, published by the American Association for Artificial Intelligence.

Unlike most planning systems, the plans or intentions formed by the robot need only be partly elaborated before it decides to act. This allows the robot to avoid overly strong expectations about the environment, overly constrained plans of action, and other forms of overcommitment common to previous planners. In addition, the robot is continuously reactive and has the ability to change its goals and intentions as situations warrant. The system has been tested with SRI's autonomous robot (Flakey) in a space station scenario involving navigation and the performance of emergency tasks.

Most existing architectures for embedded planning systems consist of a plan constructor and a plan executor. As a rule, the plan constructor formulates an entire course of action before commencing execution of the plan [Fikes and Nilsson 1971, Vere 1983, Wilkens 1985]. The plan itself is typically composed of primitive actions—that is, actions that are directly performable by the system. The rationale for this approach, of course, is to ensure that the planned sequence of actions will actually achieve the prescribed goal. As the plan is executed, the system performs these primitive actions by calling various low-level routines. Execution is usually monitored to ensure that these routines will culminate in the desired effects; if they do not, the system can return control to the plan constructor so that it may modify the existing plan appropriately.

One problem with these schemes is that, in many domains, much of the information about how best to achieve a given goal is acquired during plan execution. For example, in planning to get from home to the airport, the particular sequence of actions to be performed depends on information acquired on the way—such as which turnoff to take, which lane to get into, when to slow down or speed up, and so on. To overcome this problem, at least in part, there has been some work on developing planning systems that interleave plan formation and execution [Davis and Chien 1977, Durfee and Lesser 1986]. Such systems are better suited to uncertain worlds than the kind of system described above, as decisions can be deferred until they *have* to be made. The reason for deferring decisions is that an agent can acquire *more* information as time passes; thus, the quality of its decisions can be expected only to improve. Of course, because of the need to coordinate some activities in advance and because of practical restrictions on the amount of decision-making that can be accomodated during task execution, there are limitations on the degree to which such decisions may be deferred [Georgeff and Lansky 1987].

> — Reprinted with permission from *Proceedings of the National Conference on Artificial Intelligence (AAAI-87)*, 1987, pp. 677f., published by the American Association for Artificial Intelligence.

3.5 Monitoring Values of Measurements

Will the expert system be performing a monitoring task so that several measurements are made of the same quantity over time? If so, what is required to make the proper interpretation of these measurements?

1. **The proper interpretation of a measurement depends only on the current value of that measurement.**

2. **The proper interpretation of a measurement depends on the time course of that measurement.** (For example: *Interpretation might require knowing whether a quantity is rising or stable.*)

3. **The proper interpretation of a measurement depends on knowing which of several states the system under analysis is in when the measurement is made.** (For example: *Interpretation of a particular medical observation might require knowing whether the patient is in critical condition or in fair condition.*)

4. **The proper interpretation of a measurement requires having followed this particular case over time so that a customized set of expectations is developed. These expectations provide an understanding of the significance of this measurement for this particular case.** (For example: *A temperature of 97.8 is not unusual for this patient.*)

Evidence: Any   Type: Simulation

Current value   → Associate interpretations directly with mea-
                         surement ranges {cheap}.

Time course   → Develop primitives for querying and assert-
                         ing parameters whose values vary over
                         time.

State-dependent   → Associate interpretations with pairings of
                         states and measurement ranges.

Case-dependent   → Develop a customized set of expectations
                         adapted to the case at hand {expensive}.

Choices 1 through 4 are not mutually exclusive. For example, the VM
system monitors patients who are receiving mechanical breathing assistance, and this domain is characterized by choices 2, 3, and possibly 4.

Time Course of Measurement

In VM we have begun to experiment with mechanisms for providing
MYCIN-like systems with the ability to represent the dynamic nature
of the diagnosis and therapy process....MYCIN was designed to produce therapeutic decisions for one critical moment in a patient's hospital
course. This was extended with a "restart mechanism" that allows for
selectively updating those parameters that might change in the interval
between consultations. MYCIN can start a new consultation with the
updated information, but the results of the original consultation are lost.
In VM, three requirements are necessary to support the processing of
new time frames: (1) examining the values of historical data and conclusions, (2) determining the validity of those data, and (3) combining new
conclusions with previous conclusions.

New premise functions, which define the relationships about parameters
that can be tested when a rule is checked for validity, were created to
examine the historical data. Premise functions used in MYCIN include
tests to see if: (a) any value has been determined for a parameter, (b)
the value associated with a parameter is in a particular numerical range,
or (c) there is a particular value associated with a parameter. VM includes a series of time-related premise functions. One function examines
trends in input data over time—e.g., THE MEAN ARTERIAL PRES-
SURE DOES NOT RISE BY 15 TORR IN 15 MINUTES. A second
function determines the stability of a series of measurements, by examining the variation of measurements over a specific time period. Other

functions examine previously deduced conclusions, as in THE PATIENT HAS BEEN ON THE T-PIECE FOR GREATER THAN 30 MIN-UTES or THE PATIENT HAS NEVER BEEN ON THE T-PIECE. Functions also exist for determining changes in the state of the patient—e.g., THE PATIENT HAS TRANSITIONED FROM ASSIST MODE TO THE T-PIECE. When VM is required to check if a parameter has a particular value, it must also check to see if the value is "recent" enough to be useful.

The notion that data are reliable for only a given period of time is also used in the representation of conclusions made by the program. When the same conclusion is made in contiguous time periods (two successive evaluations of the rule set), then the conclusions are coalesced. The result is a series of intervals that specify when a parameter assumed a particular value. In the MYCIN system this information is stored as several different parameters. For example, the period when a drug was given is represented by a pair of parameters corresponding to the starting and ending times of administration. In MYCIN, if a drug was again started and stopped, a new entity—DRUG-2—would have to be created. The effect of the VM representation is to aggregate individual conclusions into *states* whose persistence denotes a meaningful interpretation of the status of the patient [Fagan, Kunz, Feigenbaum, and Osborn, 1984, pp. 420–421].

   — Buchanan/Shortliffe, *Rule-Based Expert Systems*, © 1984 by B. G. Buchanan and E. H. Shortliffe. Reprinted with permission of Addison-Wesley Publishing Co., Inc., Reading, Massachusetts.

State-Dependent Interpretation

Data are collected in different therapeutic situations, or *contexts*. In order to interpret the data properly, VM includes a model of the stages that a patient follows from ICU [Intensive Care Unit] admission through the end of the critical monitoring phase. The correct interpretation of physiologic measurements depends on knowing which stage the patient is in. The goals for intensive care are also stated in terms of these clinical contexts. The program maintains descriptions of the current and optimal ventilatory therapies for any given time [Fagan, Kunz, Feigenbaum, and Osborn, 1984, p. 398].

   — Buchanan/Shortliffe, *Rule-Based Expert Systems*, © 1984 by B. G. Buchanan and E. H. Shortliffe. Reprinted with permission of Addison-Wesley Publishing Co., Inc., Reading, Massachusetts.

Case-Dependent Expectations

Patients receiving digitalis therapy for various cardiac conditions must be monitored closely for evidence of digitalis toxicity. The ANNA system written by Silverman is one of several digitalis therapy systems written at MIT/Tufts to address this problem. A complicating feature of digitalis administration is that patients show highly variable patterns of response to the drug. Proper treatment requires an appreciation of how this particular patient has responded in the past to particular dosages. While Silverman uses the term *patient specific model* to refer to case-dependent expectations, the term is not consistently used with this meaning in descriptions of the MIT/Tufts programs. Often the term refers only to the facts known about this particular patient.

Jelliffe's programs [for administering digitalis] [Jelliffe 1968; Jelliffe, Buell, and Kalaba 1970, 1972] made use of a quantitative model that is based on the mathematical relationships between maintenance dose, renal function, weight, etc.... . This model is implemented in the form of a procedure that accepts various parameters (renal function, weight, etc) and yields the appropriate maintenance dose.... Different patients are modeled by changing these input parameters, but the (internal) procedural model remains unaltered.

Studies have indicated that there is a limit to the effectiveness of Jelliffe's programs.... . It was felt that this limit arose from the inadequacy of the modeling facilities used by these programs. Instead of using a single patient model, the system should have the ability to "*tailor-make*" a model for each patient it considers, basing its recommendations on this patient specific model.

Use of this model involves a two step process,...:

1. *Construction of a Patient Specific Model and Generation of the Initial Guess*. A *patient specific model* (PSM) is formulated based on a general model and on the answers to various questions concerning the current clinical setting. This may involve looking at a number of parameters, such as renal function, age, weight, sensitivities, and the reason for digitalization. Once the PSM has been obtained, it is used to formulate an "educated guess" at the proper level of digitalis for the patient.

2. *The feedback loop*. The second step is the refinement of the PSM in a feedback loop. Once the initial dose has been administered, the patient's response is interpreted with respect to the previously constructed PSM. Comparison of the demonstrated response to the expected response may result in a change in the PSM. For example, if no effect at all is seen, the PSM might be expanded to include the possibility of malabsorption. Once the PSM has been updated, it is used to formulate the next step in therapy.

[Silverman 1974, pp. 40–42].
— Copyright 1974, Massachusetts Institute of Technology. Reprinted by permission.

The VM expert system, which monitors patients receiving mechanical breathing assistance, did not employ case-dependent expectations. However, the following quote makes it clear that the authors of the VM expert system see case-dependent expectations as having advantages for this domain.

Knowledge about the patient could be used to "customize" the expectation limits for the individual patient. The first possibility is the use of historical information to establish *a priori* expectations based on type of surgery, age, length of time on the heart/lung machine, and presurgical pulmonary and hemodynamic status. The second type of customization could be based on the observation that patient measurements tend to run within tighter bands than the *a priori* expectations. The third type of expectation based on transient events can be used to adjust for the effects of temporary intervention by clinicians. This requires expert knowledge about the side effects of each intervention and about the variation between different classes of patients to these temporary changes [Fagan, Kunz, Feigenbaum, and Osborn 1984, pp. 418–419].
— Buchanan/Shortliffe, *Rule-Based Expert Systems*, © 1984 by B. G. Buchanan and E. H. Shortliffe. Reprinted with permission of Addison-Wesley Publishing Co., Inc., Reading, Massachusetts.

3.6 Change Invalidates Conclusions

Will the expert system be working with input data that have been entered at a variety of different times?

and

In the course of solving the problem, do events occur that are certain to invalidate old information? (For example: *A diagnosis and repair system for a computer should understand that replacing a board invalidates all observations and conclusions made about that board previously.*)

or

Is new information just generally more trustworthy than old information?

Evidence: Any   Type: Any

Invalidating events   → *Reason Explicitly about Time* and/or use a *Truth Maintenance System* {expensive}.

Decay in   → Use recency of data in conflict resolution
trustworthiness   and/or attach "expiration dates" on information.

Reason Explicitly about Time

Traditionally, temporal considerations have not played a major role in the reasoning processes of problem solving and planning systems. Systems that operate in the blocks world, for example, focus on planning and executing solutions to problems without concern to the intervals of time encompassed by these solutions. Only an implicit notion of time, as embodied in the relationships between states in a given problem space, is present. In attempting to solve problems that place time restrictions on the completion of activities and achievements of goals, however, the inadequacy of this *instantaneous time slices* approach to modeling time becomes apparent. The ability to reason about time requires an explicit representation.

Despite a recognition of this need, the explicit treatment of time in problem solving/planning systems is fairly uncommon. The AUTOPILOT system [Thorndike, McArthur, and Cammarata 1981], a special purpose, distributed planning system for guiding multiple aircraft through a common airspace, utilizes a specific notion of time in representing aircraft flight plans although this technique appears to have limited applicability. The NUDGE system [Goldstein and Roberts 1977] also takes a domain specific approach, utilizing a rich set of knowledge about the time requirements of various activities and the time preferences of specific individuals to produce a schedule of an individual's weekly activities under consideration. Vere has described a more general technique for planning within imposed time spans [Vere 1981] that associates start time *windows* and *durations* with the various activities under consideration. This temporal information is refined and propagated to other activities in the plan as the plan crystalizes. A similar approach is taken in [Fukumori 1980] in developing train schedules.

The general issue of representing and reasoning with temporal knowledge has also been considered [Bruce 1972, Kahn and Gorry 1977, Allen 1981a, Villain 1982], although primarily in the context of natural language comprehension and generation. These efforts focused on providing schemes for efficiently organizing a body of temporal knowledge and deductive methods that exploit these representations in responding

to queries. Some recent proposals [Allen 1981b; McDermott, D., 1982] have attempted to place these temporal models within a larger framework in which plans and actions can be expressed. [p. 2]
— Reprinted with permisssion from Smith, S. F. *Exploiting Temporal Knowledge to Organize Constraints*. CMU-RI-TR-83-12, The Robotics Institute, Carnegie-Mellon University, July 1983.

Decay in Trustworthiness

Any value associated with a measured parameter that was concluded too long ago is considered to be unknown and, therefore, no longer useful in the reasoning mechanism. This is meant to be a first approximation to our intuition that confidence in an interpretation decays over time unless it is reinforced by new observations. [Fagan, Kunz, Feigenbaum, and Osborn 1984, p. 416]
— Buchanan/Shortliffe, *Rule-Based Expert Systems*, © 1984 by B. G. Buchanan and E. H. Shortliffe. Reprinted with permission of Addison-Wesley Publishing Co., Inc., Reading, Massachusetts.

3.7 Creating New Relationships

Are all the kinds of relationships the expert system will have to reason about known at program-design time?

or

Will the expert system need to create new kinds of relationships in the process of solving a problem? (For example: *new rules, new concepts, new slots, or new links.*)

Evidence: Any   Type: Constructed, simulation

Create new
relationships

→ Use *Meta-Level Reasoning* to generate new relationships. For example, new rules can be developed by using a version of *Resolution* that allows *Middle-out Reasoning*; the *Linear Input Strategy* is one such version {expensive}.

Evidence: Moderate, powerful

The DART expert system [Genesereth 1982] is an example of where the program creates new rules during its reasoning. The DART system devises tests to diagnose faulty hardware [Genesereth 1983, p. 123]. An example of a test would be "if a 1 is put on input port a, then the output should be 0." These tests are rules, and the following quote shows how the Middle-out Reasoning provided by Resolution can derive them.

> In addition to top-down and bottom-out inference, resolution includes middle-out reasoning with Horn clauses. The resolvent of the two clauses
>
> $$\underline{\text{Fallible}(x)} \leftarrow \text{Human}(x)$$
> $$\text{Mortal}(x) \leftarrow \underline{\text{Fallible}(x)}$$
>
> for example, is the clause Mortal(x) $\leftarrow$ Human(x).
>
> Middle-out reasoning can also be applied to different copies of the same clause. From two copies of the definition of ancestor, for example
>
> $$\text{Ancestor}(x,y) \leftarrow \underline{\text{Ancestor}(x,z)}, \text{Ancestor}(z,y)$$
> $$\underline{\text{Ancestor}(u,v)} \leftarrow \text{Ancestor}(u,w), \text{Ancestor}(w,v)$$
>
> we can derive the resolvent
>
> $$\text{Ancestor}(x,y) \leftarrow \text{Ancestor}(x,w), \text{Ancestor}(w,z), \text{Ancestor}(z,y)$$
>
> [pp. 150–151].
> — Reprinted by permission of the publisher from *Logic for Problem Solving* by R. Kowalski. Copyright 1979 by Elsevier Science Publishing Co., Inc.

3.8 Falsifying Assumptions

Does making progress on problems in this domain typically require making assumptions?

and

Is it possible that the assumptions will be discovered to be false only after many other conclusions have been derived on the basis of these assumptions?

and

Is there no way to establish a "time limit" such that if an assumption is really false, it will be discovered by then?

Evidence: Weak, moderate   Type: Constructed, simulation

Unclear when assumptions will be falsified	→ Use a *Truth Maintenance System* to record the dependencies between assumptions and conclusions. *Dependency-Directed Backtracking* can use these dependencies to remove conclusions based on false assumptions.
Assumptions revocable only during a well-defined period	→ *Chronological Backtracking*

Chronological Backtracking and Truth Maintenance systems have similar abilities to remove the consequences of an assumption that turn out to be false. They differ in that Truth Maintenance allows assumptions and their consequences to be revoked at any point, whereas Backtracking must eventually accept or reject an assumption. Once a Chronological Backtracking scheme concludes that it has found a solution, there is no easy way to remove the consequences of an assumption that turns out to be false. This difference is the result of different methods for storing dependencies. Chronological Backtracking stores dependencies in a control stack or other form of temporary storage, whereas Truth Maintenance employs permanent data structures. The EL system [Stallman and Sussman 1977] is an example of an expert system that has used Truth Maintenance to recover from erroneous assumptions.

Truth Maintenance Systems

The dependency network makes it easy to explore hypothetical situations. We can place a value in some terminal and see what values propagate from it. When we are through with this exploration, we can remove the value at the terminal, and everything that depends on it will be removed as well, courtesy of the dependency network, which has done all of the necessary record keeping. Consequently, we can easily discover the answer to some questions by simulation: we can get the device to a particular state and then very carefully explore multiple alternative futures from that point [Davis and Shrobe 1983, p. 78].

— © 1983 by IEEE. Reprinted by permission.

4 The Expert System's Environment

An expert system must be well matched to its operational environment to be useful. One important characteristic of the environment is the amount of information or guidance it provides to the expert system. Expert systems provide assistance to their users, but in order to do so, the expert systems themselves generally need assistance in the form of information or guidance. The amount of assistance that an expert system can rely on without compromising its usefulness is an issue that has a significant impact on the design of an expert system. The following design guideline is concerned with this issue.

4.1 Cooperation from Source of Inputs

What is the nature of the environment that provides inputs to the expert system?

1. Cooperative and knowledgeable users will provide inputs.

2. Users are cooperative, but not always knowledgeable. That is, some questions are likely to receive unreliable answers when posed to certain users.

3. **The environment is hostile and might mislead the expert system with false inputs.** (For example: *Enemy submarines have no interest in helping an expert system locate them via the acoustic signals they emit and might try to hide by emitting no signals or camouflage their presence by emitting misleading signals.*)

4. **Neutral environment that is a source of data, but does not try to influence the expert system one way or another.**

	Evidence: Any Type: Any
Both Cooperative and Knowledgeable	→ Accept the information that is input as accurate and complete.
Not Always Knowledgeable	→ Tailor information gathering to the knowledge level of individual user. *or* Allow the users to indicate how certain they are that their answers are correct. *or* Apply more consistency checks when users are less knowledgeable.
Hostile	→ Expend much effort in *Consistency Checking*, set up procedures to look for evidence of deception, *Reason Explicitly about Uncertainty*, use *Endorsement-Based Approaches* to try to resolve uncertainties, and so on.
Neutral	→ Expend moderate effort on *Consistency Checking*.

This guideline suggests that one extreme environment is the misleading information arising from deception in military settings and another extreme environment is the reliable information provided by cooperative and knowledgeable users. However, if guidance rather than information is at issue, such as in Guideline 4.2, then an extreme case of accommodation is a division of labor between user and machine where the user makes all the critical decisions. The expert system might display the decision options and then trace the consequences of the user's decisions. With this kind of arrangement, the expert system is not capable of solving the entire problem by itself and is dependent on guidance from a very accommodating environment; that is, a competent user to whom it can defer decisions.

4.1.1 Support for Example Guideline 4.1

Cooperative and Knowledgeable

The [MYCIN] consultation model assumes a cooperative and knowledgeable user. We attempted to make the system so robust that a user cannot cause an unrecoverable error by mistake. But the designers of any knowledge base still have to anticipate synonyms and strange paths through the rules because we know of no safeguards against malice and ignorance. Some medically impossible values are still not caught by MYCIN.[1] If users are cooperative enough to be careful about the medical correctness of what they type, MYCIN's implementation of the consulation model is robust enough to be helpful [Buchanan and Shortliffe 1984, p. 692].

> — Buchanan/Shortliffe, *Rule-Based Expert Systems*, © 1984 by B. G. Buchanan and E. H. Shortliffe. Reprinted with permission of Addison-Wesley Publishing Co., Inc., Reading, Massachusetts.

Not Always Knowledgeable

Accuracy in recognition of lymph node features is highly dependent on the level of expertise of the physician. By allowing for this, the PATHFINDER expert system minimizes the collection of potentially inaccurate data.

The collection of accurate data is especially important in reasoning about lymphatic pathology. Discussions with expert hematopathologists about the expertise-dependent problems with the recognition and quantification of lymph node features suggested that the questions selected by PATHFINDER at each point in a case should be tailored to different levels of user expertise. We have found that the need for customizing question-generation and inference to a user's expertise to minimize the collection of inaccurate data is an important yet relatively unexplored issue. Such methods could enable medical expert systems to adapt the

---

[1]For example, John McCarthy (maliciously) told MYCIN that the site of a culture was amniotic fluid—for a male patient—and MYCIN incorrectly accepted it [McCarthy 1984]. Nonmedical users...have found similar "far out" bugs as a consequence of sheer ignorance of medicine.

selection of questions to maximize the accuracy of the inference process [Horvitz, Heckerman, Nathwani, and Fagan 1984, p. 634].

— © 1984 by IEEE. Reprinted by permission.

4.2   User–System Partnership

Is the problem either a design problem or a planning problem?

and

Is there no time pressure on either the expert system or the user?

and

Do some of the decisions made in the design or plan have far-reaching implications?

and

Will the expert system run on hardware that can support fast graphics or other high-bandwidth communications?

Evidence: Any   Type: Constructed

Yes → Consider the feasibility of a division of labor between user and machine where the user makes the critical decisions. The expert system can display the decision options for the user and trace the consequences of the user's decisions whenever possible.

No → Automate the entire solution process.

The graphics capabilities available on Lisp Machines and other advanced workstations allow for efficient dialogue between user and machine, and this can tip the balance in favor of User–Machine Partnerships as opposed to total automation. For example, the MOLGEN expert systems [Stefik 1981a,b; Friedland and Iwasaki 1985] were originally developed on a time-shared mainframe computer. Communicating alternatives to the designer of molecular genetics experiments via graphics was not a feasible option—it would have taken too long to generate the required graphics objects.

However, when a commercial product was developed later to assist in planning genetics experiments, it took advantage of Lisp Machine graphics to present an analysis of design alternatives to the user. The user would select an alternative, and then the expert system would determine the next choice point for the user and show those alternatives. The design process continues in this way with the system presenting the detailed options and the human making the decisions. The following quote presents another example of this division of labor in the ISIS system, which assists users in job-shop scheduling.

Whether a division of labor is appropriate depends on the time pressures involved in the task. A busy pilot in an airplane cockpit cannot take time out whenever the expert system is faced with a critical decision, so an interactive program in that environment cannot be expected to perform time-critical functions. In the slower paced environment of the command headquarters, however, an expert system to aid in strategic planning would be practical even if it had to wait for the users of the program to make certain critical decisions.

> The discussion of the previous two sections centered on the automatic generation of job shop schedules via constraint-directed search. As mentioned at the outset, ISIS also provides the user with the capability to interactively construct and alter schedules. In this capacity, ISIS plays the role of an intelligent assistant, using its constraint knowledge to maintain the consistency of the schedule under development and identify scheduling decisions that result in poorly satisfied constraints [p. 18].
> — Reprinted with permission from Fox, M. S., Allen, B. P., Smith, S. F., and Strohm, G. A. *ISIS: A constraint-directed reasoning approach to job shop scheduling.* CMU-RI-TR-83-8, The Robotics Institute, Carnegie-Mellon University, Pittsburgh, PA, 1983.

4.3 Incomplete Information

Will the expert system often have only incomplete knowledge of the facts of the problem? That is, does the input data constrain the facts of the problem to a range of possibilities without saying specifically which of the possibilities is actually the case? (For example: *"Division X are not in their barracks"* does not say where this division is actually located.*)

and

Is there limited access to information in this environment, so that these uncertainties about the facts of the case cannot be resolved

simply by asking for the information? (For example: *The expert system may be trying to deduce enemy intentions from intelligence data.*)

and

Is it important to achieve as complete an understanding of the actual facts of the case as is possible?

Evidence: Any   Type: Any

Yes → Adopt or develop methods for representing and reasoning with incomplete information. For example, represent the information in *First-Order Logic* (also known as *Predicate Calculus*) and use *Resolution* to generate inferences {expensive}.

No → Use inference mechanisms that achieve computational efficiency by sacrificing the ability to represent and reason with incomplete knowledge. For example, represent the knowledge using *Horn Clauses* and use *PROLOG* to derive inferences. Other common representational schemes (*Rules, Frames, Semantic Nets,* etc.) usually have minimal ability to represent and reason with incomplete knowledge.

Three of the following four quotes are by authors (Levesque, Brachman, and Fikes) connected with the KRYPTON project. Representing incomplete knowledge was one of the concerns of this project.

First-Order Logic

In KR [Knowledge Representation], on the other hand, the domains being characterized are usually finite. The power of FOL [First-Order Logic] is used not so much to deal with infinities, but to deal with *incomplete knowledge* [Levesque 1982]. Consider the kind of facts[2] that might be represented using FOL:

a. ¬ Student(john).
  This sentence says that John is not a student without saying what John is.

---

[2]The use of FOL to capture *terminology* or laws is somewhat different. See Levesque [1982] for details.

b. Parent(sue,bill) ∨ Parent(sue,george).
   This sentence says that either Bill or George is a parent of Sue, but does not specify which.

c. ∃x Cousin(bill,x) ∧ Male(x).
   This sentence says that Bill has at least one male cousin but does not say who that cousin is.

d. ∀x Friend(george,x) ⊃ ∃y Child(x,y).
   This sentence says that all of George's friends have children without saying who those friends or their children are or even if there are any.

The main feature of these examples is that FOL is not used to capture complex details about the domain, but to avoid having to represent details that may not be known. *The expressive power of FOL determines not so much what can be said, but what can be left unsaid.*

For a system that has to be able to acquire knowledge in a piecemeal fashion, there may be no alternative to using all of FOL. But if we can restrict the kind of incompleteness that has to be dealt with, we can also avoid having to use the full expressiveness of FOL. This in turn might lead to a more manageable inference procedure [Levesque 1984, p. 146].
  — Levesque, H. J. A fundamental tradeoff in knowledge representation and reasoning. *Proceedings of the Fourth Conference of the Canadian Society for Computational Studies of Intelligence*, London, Ontario, 1984, pp. 141–152. Copyright 1984, Canadian Society for Computational Studies of Intelligence. Reprinted by permission.

Horn Clauses

The following quote points out that the interpretation of negation in PROLOG as "failure to prove" makes it impossible to use negation to express incomplete information.

The meta-language interpretation of "only-if" entails the interpretation of negation as failure:

> not–P holds
>
> if the if–halves of definitions fail to establish P.

The language of Horn clauses augmented with negation as failure provides a powerful extension of the language of Horn clauses alone. It is easy to implement, efficient to use and has much of the expressive power of the full standard form of logic. It is an important feature of all PROLOG implementations that they either provide the negation operator explicitly or else they provide means for defining it.

Clark has shown that Horn clauses with negation interpreted as failure do not have the full power of negation in the standard form of logic [pp. 219f.].

　　— Reprinted by permission of the publisher from *Logic for Problem Solving* by R. Kowalski. Copyright 1979, Elsevier Science Publishing Co., Inc.

The footnote of the following quote argues that the Horn Clause form employed in PROLOG also makes it impossible to use disjunction and existential quantification to express incomplete information.

The net result of these restrictions is a KB [Knowledge Base] that once again has complete knowledge of the world (within a given language), but this time, may require inference to answer questions.[3] The reasoning in this case is the *execution* of the logic program [Levesque 1984, p. 148].

　　— Levesque, H. J. A fundamental tradeoff in knowledge representation and reasoning. *Proceedings of the Fourth Conference of the Canadian Society for Computational Studies of Intelligence*, London, Ontario, 1984, pp. 141– 152. Copyright 1984, Canadian Society for Computational Studies of Intelligence. Reprinted by permission.

Frames

Instantiation (filling in the slots of a frame), the basic form of assertion in frame systems, makes expressions of incomplete knowledge either difficult or impossible. For example, a statement such as "either Elsie or Bessie is the cow standing in Farmer Jones's field" cannot be made in a typical assertional frame system [Brachman, Fikes, and Levesque 1983b, p. 68].

4.4　Explain Situation or Explain Reasoning

Should the explanations that the expert system provides concentrate on accounting for details of the situation under analysis? (For example: *Concentrate on explaining the dependencies between observed findings.*)

　　or

---

[3]Notice that it is impossible to state in a KB of this form that $(p \lor q)$ is true without saying which, or that $\exists x P(x)$ is true without saying what that x is.

Is it sufficient to get explanations that tell how the expert system arrived at its answer?

Evidence: Any   Type: Any

Explain the situation → *Causal Models* or *Blackboards*

Type: Constructed, simulation

Explain the reasoning → *Rules*; see Guideline 4.5

Type: Preenumerated, constructed

The first quote contrasts the explanatory capabilities of systems that rely on rules of evidence with the explanatory capabilities of systems that either construct causal paths (referred to as "mediated" systems in the quote) or rely on a symbolic simulation (referred to as "dynamic" systems).

> In discussing the explanation capabilities of a diagnostic system, it is useful to distinguish explanations which provide justifications for a diagnostic conclusion, from those which provide a warrant. A justification cites the facts used as evidence in coming to a diagnosis, while a warrant provides a reason for the evidential significance of these facts. For instance, accepting the hypothesis that a salt formation is being drilled would be justified in part by reference to the observation that there had been an increase in chlorides. That an increase in chlorides counts as evidence for this judgement is warranted by noting that salt is composed of chlorides, it dissolves in water, and after dissolution, the free chlorides can be observed given the method used.
>
> MUD is able to provide a justification for its diagnostic conclusions using a trace of the evidence it considered during its evaluation procedures. It has no straightforward way to warrant the use of this evidence. Both the **mediated** and **dynamic** approaches offer a more obvious potential for generating warrants. Both can offer a trace of the causal path from initiating cause to observed symptoms. This can provide the warrant for the significance of evidential considerations, as long as the considerations are junctures on the path [p. 26].
>
> — Kahn, G. On when diagnostic systems want to do without causal knowledge. In *ECAI-84: Advances in Artificial Intelligence*, T. O'Shea (ed.). Amsterdam: Elsevier, 1984, pp. 21–30. Copyright 1984, Elsevier Science Publishers B.V.

The following quote reiterates that causal information is important for explaining real-world situations. This is clearly a goal for SOPHIE-III because in addition to doing diagnosis, it also tutored students on how to troubleshoot electronic devices.

> The kinds of simulators most often used in electronics rely on "relaxation" methods for solving the system of equations characterizing circuit behavior. Although these techniques are extraordinarily powerful, the intermediate solution states they pass through bear little resemblance to any kind of causality underlying the circuit. Indeed, the circuit itself is represented as a set of constraints and the sought-after behavior is that which simultaneously satisfies all the given constraints. Nevertheless, students and experts alike can best understand a circuit, and remember their understanding, if an "explanation" reveals some underlying causality. Thus, to be able to get maximal pedagogical leverage from the simulation, we need to find ways of getting causal information [Brown, Burton, and de Kleer 1982, p. 247].
>
> — Copyright 1982, Academic Press. Reprinted by permission.

Both MYCIN and TEIRESIAS provide explanations that describe the program's reasoning process.

> There are essential assumptions as well in the use of this formalism as the basis for an interactive system. First, our explanation capabilities... rest on the assumption that display of either a rule or some segment of the control flow is a reasonable explanation of system behavior [p. 31].
>
> — Davis, R., Buchanan, B. G., and Shortliffe, E. H. Production rules as a representation for a knowledge-based consultation program. *Artificial Intelligence, 8* (1977). Copyright 1977, Elsevier Science Publishers B.V.

The SU/X program (also called HASP/SIAP) interprets data from underwater acoustic sensors to determine ship positions. A satisfactory explanation must indicate why the program has concluded that a particular ship is in a particular position. Given the broad scope of attention required to successfully disentangle the overlapping acoustic signals, a summary of important evidence for a single ship must be collected from widely separated parts of the program's reasoning trace. Further discussion of this approach to explanation can be found in Nii, Feigenbaum, Anton, and Rockmore [1982, pp. 32f.].

> The design of appropriate explanations for the user takes an interesting twist in SU/X. The situation/hypothesis unfolds piecemeal over time,

but the "appropriate" explanation for the user is one that focuses on individual objects over time. Thus the appropriate explanation must be synthesized from a history of all the events that led up to the current hypothesis. Contrast this with the MYCIN–TEIRESIAS reporting of rule invocations in the construction of the reasoning chain [Feigenbaum 1977, pp. 1025f.].

— © 1977 Edward A. Feigenbaum.

4.5 Alternative Explanations of Reasoning

Which of the following ways of explaining how the expert system arrived at its answer will be required?

1. **Users will want to know what knowledge was used to reach this conclusion.**

2. **Users will want to know why that knowledge was used instead of some other knowledge.** (That is: *They may have questions about how the inference engine works.*)

3. **Users will want a justification or explanation of the knowledge itself.** (For example: *Why is gram stain so important in diagnosing infectious diseases?*)

Evidence: Any   Type: Any

What knowledge	→ Backtrace in pseudo-English as in EMY-CIN.
Why not some other knowledge	→ Use "canned" descriptions of the reasoning processes employed {cheap}. *or* Rely on the system's *Meta-Knowledge* about its own processing strategies to provide an explanation that specifically addresses the case under discussion {expensive}.

Defend the knowledge → Store and retrieve a text string of justifying documentation {cheap}.

or

Use an automatic programmer to derive a set of rules from a deep model of the domain. The expert system can then use these derivations to help justify the rules {expensive}.

or

Place information in the knowledge base by hand that records the principles that support and explain the rules. The expert system can then use this information to help justify the rules.

Justifications from Canned Text versus Justifications from Automatic Compilation

```
WHAT IS THE LEVEL OF SERUM CALCIUM?

ENTER NUMERICAL VALUE ===> why?
```

(The user types 'why' indicating that he questions why he is being asked to supply the value of serum calcium.)

```
MY GOAL IS TO BEGIN THERAPY. ONE STEP IN DOING THAT IS TO CHECK
SENSITIVITIES.
I AM NOW TRYING TO CHECK SENSITIVITY DUE TO CALCIUM.
```

Figure 4.1. Explanation produced by direct translation. Reprinted with permission from Swartout, W. *Explainable Expert Systems.* USC/ Information Sciences Institute, Marina del Rey, CA, October 1983.

Figure 4.1 shows an explanation produced by just translating the program stack of an early version of the Digitalis Advisor [Swartout 1977]. While the code might do the correct thing, and while such an explanation might suggest what the Digitalis Advisor does, it does not tell us why the actions are reasonable, nor does it tell us what ill effects might arise from the interaction of digitalis and high serum calcium. Indeed, none of this information is even represented in the system.

The issue then is how to capture the expert system builder's reasoning (and the domain knowledge needed to support it) in a principled fashion. One way would be to require the system builder to annotate the system during creation with text strings justifying the system's methods. The text strings would then be displayed during execution in response

to queries [Chandrasekaran and Mittal 1982]. Clearly, the problem with this approach is that there is no way to assure that the justifications provided accurately reflect what the code actually does. This problem is exacerbated by program maintenance and evolution. Our approach in the XPLAIN system was to use an automatic programmer to create an expert system from deep knowledge about the domain. The automatic programmer provided us with a principled way of modeling the process of creating an expert system. As it created an expert system, its reasoning was recorded in a machine readable form and was used to provide machine produced justifications of the expert system's performance. We selected the domain of digitalis therapy as a testbed for our approach [Swartout 1983, p. 2].
— Reprinted by permission of author.

Hand-Code Support Knowledge for Justification

The following two quotes describe approaches to explanation taken in the GUIDON system. A detailed description of GUIDON can be found in Clancey [1987].

We have most recently used the MYCIN knowledge base as the foundation of a tutorial system, called GUIDON. The goal of this project is to study the problem of transferring the expertise of MYCIN-like systems to a student. It is argued in this paper that MYCIN-like rule-based expert systems constitute a good basis for tutorial programs, but they are not sufficient in themselves for making knowledge accessible to a student.

In GUIDON we have augmented the performance knowledge of rules by adding two other levels: a "support level" to justify individual rules, and an "abstraction level" to organize rules into patterns [pp. 201–202].

The support tier of the knowledge base consists of annotations to the rules and the factors used by them.[4] For example, there are canned-text descriptions of every laboratory test in the MYCIN domain, including, for instance, remarks about how the test should be performed. Mechanism descriptions provided by the domain expert are used to provide some explanation of a rule beyond the canned text of the justification. For the infectious disease domain of MYCIN, they indicate how a given factor leads to a particular infection with particular organisms by stating the origin of the organism and the favorable conditions for its growth at the site of infection. Thus, the frame associated with the factor "a seriously burned patient" shows that the organisms originate in the air

[4]Rule justifications, author and edit date were first proposed by Davis [1976] as knowledge base maintenance records.

and grow in the exposed tissue of a burn, resulting in a frequently fatal infection.

The abstraction tier of the knowledge base represents patterns in the performance knowledge. For example, a rule schema is a description of a kind of rule: a pattern of preconditions that appears in the premise, the goal concluded about, and the context of its application. The schema and a canned-text annotation of its significance are formalized in the MYCIN knowledge base by a physician expert. This schema is used by the tutor to "subtract off" the rule preconditions common to all rules of the type, leaving behind the factors that are specific to this particular rule, i.e., the "key factors" of this rule.

Rule models [Davis 1976] are program-generated patterns that represent the typical clusters of factors in the expert's rules. Unlike rule schemas, rule models do not necessarily correspond to domain concepts, though they do represent factors that tend to appear together in domain arguments (rules). An example from the MYCIN data base shows that the gram stain of an organism and its morphology tend to appear together in rules for determining the identity of an organism. Because rule models capture the factors that most commonly appear in rules for pursuing a goal, we are experimenting with their use as a form of "orientation" for naive students [Clancey 1982, pp. 211–213].
— Copyright 1982, Academic Press London. Reprinted by permission.

Use Meta-Knowledge to Explain Processing

Meta-knowledge of the representation and application of d-rules [domain rules] plays an important part in t-rules [tutoring rules]. For example, ... GUIDON uses function templates[5] to "read" d-rule 578 and discovers that the type of the infection is a subgoal that needs to be completed before the d-rule can be applied. This capability to examine the domain knowledge and reason about its use enables GUIDON to make multiple use of any given production rule during the tutorial session. Here are some of the uses we have implemented.

1. Examine the rule (if it was tried in the consultation) and determine the subgoals that needed to be achieved before it could be applied; if the rule failed to apply, determine all possible ways this could be determined (perhaps more than one precondition is false).

2. Examine the state of application of the rule during a tutorial interaction (what more needs to be done before it can be applied?) and choose an appropriate method of presentation.

---

[5]A function's template "indicates the order and generic type of arguments in a typical call of that function" [Davis and Buchanan, 1977, p. 924].

3. Generate different questions for the student.

4. Use the rule (and variations of it) to understand a student's hypothesis.

5. Summarize arguments using the rule by extracting the "key point" it addresses [Clancey 1982, pp. 213f.].

— Copyright 1982, Academic Press London. Reprinted by permission.

4.6 Order of Questions

Will the expert system gather its information from users?

and

Are there strong expectations on the part of the users that questions will be asked in a particular order?

Evidence: Any   Type: Any

Yes → Use a reasoning strategy such as *Depth-First Search* that is fairly natural for users.
or
Separate the questioning strategy from the reasoning strategy.

No → Gather information in whatever order is most convenient for the reasoning strategy.

The following quote argues that Depth-First Search appears more natural to users than Best-First Search.

PERMAID originally used A*-like best-first search but was modified to use depth-first search because early results indicated that FSEs [field service engineers] tend to do depth-first troubleshooting and find it difficult to understand why the system "jumps around" while doing best-first search [Rolston 1987, pp. 153f.].
— © 1987 by IEEE. Reprinted by permission.

While Depth-First Search proved satisfactory in PERMAID, the following two quotes illustrate the fact that users are sometimes unhappy with the ordering of questions that is most convenient for the Depth-First, Backward-Chaining Reasoning used in MYCIN.

The MYCIN structure performs inference by backward chaining through a set of rules until a point is reached at which no further backup is possible and the user must be asked to supply information. One of the properties of the backward chaining control structure is that both the selection and the order of questions to be asked the user is determined dynamically during the consultation. While this is certainly preferable to asking a fixed set of sometimes absurd questions, the variable ordering of questioning has a severe drawback with regard to the way physicians organize their knowledge of a patient. Customarily, in presenting a case, physicians cluster the evidence under headings such as "chief complaint," "history of present illness," and "past medical history." They use this organization as a heuristic for managing their knowledge about the patient to ensure that nothing is forgotten or left out.

With the backward chaining control structure, however, the grouping of questions is determined by the order of appearance of the parameters or variables in rules. Hence, questions about the chief complaint and present illness may be interspersed with questions about prior history of the patient or other members of the patient's family. While the prompting nature of the questions probably ensures that physicians do not forget or omit relevant information, they nevertheless find the ordering of questions disconcerting [Brooks and Heiser 1980, p. 477].
— © 1980 by IEEE. Reprinted by permission.

One way to separate question asking from the inference mechanism is to group questions into sets of related questions and then ask all the questions in the set whenever the reasoning strategy requires the answer to any one of them.

Physicians using the evolving system began to complain that MYCIN did not ask questions in the order they were used to. For example, they indicated it was standard practice to discuss the site, timing, and method of collection for a culture as soon as it was first mentioned. Thus we created a set of parameters called the MAINPROPS for each prototypical context.[6] The values of these parameters were automatically asked for when a context was first created, thereby providing the kind of focused questioning with which physicians felt most comfortable. The benefit was in creating a more natural sequence of questions. The risk was in asking a few more questions than might be logically necessary for some cases. This was a departure from the pure production system approach of asking questions only when the information was needed for evaluating the premise of a rule [Buchanan and Shortliffe 1984, p. 60].
— Buchanan/Shortliffe, *Rule-Based Expert Systems*, © 1984 by B. G. Buchanan and E. H. Shortliffe. Reprinted with permission of Addison-Wesley Publishing Co., Inc., Reading, Massachusetts.

---

[6]This name was later changed to INITIALDATA in EMYCIN systems.

The following quote discusses ARBY's use of an Interaction Manager, separate from the inference mechanism, to oversee the user interaction (ARBY is a diagnosis expert system for large electronic systems).

> The basic structure which controls the user interaction is an interaction manager, IM, and a set of interaction frames, IFs. An IF is a discrete unit of interaction with the user which, when it terminates, results in the addition of assertions to the database. A very simple IF might consist of asking the user a multiple choice question and, depending on the answer, placing just a single assertion into the database. A more complex IF might instruct the user step by step to run some complicated equipment test and then place different assertions into the database to record the results of the test.
>
> In general, however, just asking for the information in the order determined by the inference system will not result in an acceptable order of questions from the user's standpoint. The questions might have logical prerequisites which are not yet satisfied or the questions might not occur in the order to which the user is accustomed. To insure the satisfaction of these constraints, the Interaction Frame manager requires that an IF be explicitly enabled before it can be invoked. In the database, this is indicated by assertions of the form:
>
> (want ⟨IF⟩ ⟨arguments⟩)
>
> To insure, for example, that the status of switch 17 is asked about only after it has been determined that the level of amplitude modulation is high, rules of the following form could be written:
>
> (← (want IF23 17)(modulation-level high))
>
> There are also assertions for indicating that an IF has already been run and for indicating that an IF may be run whenever needed. This combination gives the interaction manager considerable power in reasoning about and optimizing the structure of interactions with the users [McDermott, D. and Brooks 1982].
> — Reprinted with permission from *Proceedings of the National Conference on Artificial Intelligence*, 1982, p. 372, published by the American Association for Artificial Intelligence.

Separating the questioning strategy from the reasoning strategy has implications for reasoning control. This is discussed in the following quote that discusses the Interviewer/Reasoner model employed in the ONCOCIN system, which assists physicians in adminstering chemotherapy treatment to cancer patients.

In order to work effectively as a background process, the Reasoner should be primarily data-driven. A goal-directed system usually needs specific pieces of information at unpredictable times. A goal-directed Reasoner would therefore need to direct the information-gathering process, and the Interviewer/Reasoner model would gain nothing. For the model to be useful, the Interviewer must be able to gather information independently of the reasoning process. For example, this is possible for consulting systems which form conclusions from relatively standard data sets as they are entered [Gerring, Shortliffe, and van Melle 1982].

— Reprinted with permission from *AI Magazine*, 1982, p. 25, published by the American Association for Artificial Intelligence.

4.7 Initiative in Interaction

Will the expert system's input data come from interaction with users?

and

Are the inputs that the expert system requires best communicated by menu selections or short natural-language inputs from the user in response to questions from the expert system? (That is: *The user will not be able to volunteer information out of sequence.*)

or

Would it be reasonable to expect users to volunteer all the required input data by filling in forms or templates with whatever information they have access to or think is relevant?

Evidence: Any   Type: Any

Respond to system   → *Goal-Driven Reasoning*
questions

User volunteered   → *Data-Driven Reasoning*

Mixed-initiative   → Combine *Goal-Driven Reasoning* and *Data-Driven Reasoning*.

Respond to System Questions

The program [MYCIN] controls the dialogue, much as a human consultant does, by asking for specific items of data about the problem at hand. Thus the system can understand short English responses to its questions because it knows what answers are reasonable at each point in the dialogue. Moreover, it can ask for as much—and only as much—information as is relevant. Also, the knowledge base can be highly specialized because the context of the consultation can be carefully controlled.

A disadvantage of the consultation model as implemented in MYCIN, however, is that it prevents a user from volunteering pertinent data [Buchanan and Shortliffe 1984, p. 691].

> — Buchanan/Shortliffe, *Rule-Based Expert Systems*, © 1984 by B. G. Buchanan and E. H. Shortliffe. Reprinted with permission of Addison-Wesley Publishing Co., Inc., Reading, Massachusetts.

User Volunteered

An important evaluative issue that we are accordingly investigating is whether ONCOCIN encourages more complete and accurate recording of the flow sheet data despite the user's ability to skip entries if he or she wishes to do so. Users may enter data into the flow sheet format in whatever order they prefer, skipping forward or backward and changing current or old answers. This approach is radically different from that used in MYCIN in that the physician decides what information to enter and the reasoning can proceed in a data-directed fashion. Data entry in a flow sheet format avoids the problems of natural language understanding that prevented this approach in MYCIN [Buchanan and Shortliffe 1984, p. 606].

> — Buchanan/Shortliffe, *Rule-Based Expert Systems*, © 1984 by B. G. Buchanan and E. H. Shortliffe. Reprinted with permission of Addison-Wesley Publishing Co., Inc., Reading, Massachusetts.

4.8 Frequency of Device Changes

Will the expert system be solving a diagnosis problem?

and

Does the system being diagnosed undergo frequent design changes?

Evidence: Any   Type: Any

Yes → Rely on *Information about the Correct Behavior* of the system.

No → Rely on *Information about the Incorrect Behavior* of the system.

The following quote gives arguments for modeling the correct behavior of electronic hardware in order to diagnose malfunctions. For this application there is detailed knowledge available about the intended behavior of the hardware and there is a high likelihood of design changes. By contrast, expert systems for medical diagnosis have generally relied on detailed knowledge about the ways in which the human body can malfunction. For this application there is an unchanging design for the device in question—the human body.

Even in the area of diagnosing electronic hardware there are low-level components such as transistors and capacitors whose design is essentially fixed. SOPHIE-III, a system that diagnoses hardware faults, relies on knowledge of the characteristic ways in which these components can malfunction [Brown, Burton, and de Kleer 1982].

A system based on reasoning from first principles is easier to construct because there is a way of systematically enumerating the required knowledge: the structure and behavior of the device. A system based on empirical associations is more difficult to construct because the character of the knowledge makes it necessary to extract the rules on a case-by-case basis. To the extent that the knowledge is a distillation of the expert's experience, the best we can do is to assemble a representative collection of cases and ask an expert for the rules dealing with each case. No more systematic method of collecting rules is available and the process often continues for an extended period of time. This time lag is a particular problem in dealing with electronic hardware: the time necessary to accumulate the relevant experience is beginning to be longer than the design cycle for the next model of the machine.

A system based on reasoning from first principles is also easier to maintain, since modifications to the machine design are relatively easy to accommodate. We can update the structure and behavior specifications for each modified component, rather than having to determine how each change should modify the overall behavior and the troubleshooting strategy [pp. 390–391].

— Davis, R. Diagnostic reasoning based on structure and behavior. *Artificial Intelligence*, 1984, *24*. Copyright 1984, Elsevier Science Publishers B.V.

5 Computational Efficiency

Many expert systems operate in domains where a combinatorial explosion of possibilities will defeat them if they do not expend their efforts intelligently. Guideline 5.1 illustrates a variety of approaches to deciding what to do next to ensure that problems are solved within the constraints imposed by resource limitations.

5.1 Choice of Next Action

Is there a fixed order of subtasks that solves most problems in this domain?

or

Are the potential lines of reasoning few enough that the expert system can afford to investigate them in the order that is most convenient for the reasoning strategy?

or

Do experts routinely use their knowledge of the domain to make good choices of subproblems to work on next?

or

Will the expert system need to estimate the costs and benefits expected from invoking a line of reasoning so as to best allocate computational resources among a wide range of possible lines of reasoning?

Evidence: Any   Type: Constructed

Fixed order of tasks	→ Hard-wire the flow of control as in procedural programming languages or the *Match* strategy {cheap}.
At the convenience of the reasoning strategy	→ General-purpose search strategies, such as *Forward-Chaining*, *Backward-Chaining*, and *Means-Ends* {cheap}.
Domain knowledge determines next task	→ Use *Control-Rules* that embody domain knowledge to reorder the *Agenda*, set focus tasks, or invoke rule sets.
Estimate costs and benefits	→ Devise an *Intelligent Scheduler* to order tasks on an *Agenda* according to their expected benefits. *Meta-Knowledge* is required about the costs and benefits associated with potential lines of reasoning {expensive}.

This guideline contrasts various global strategies for directing the problem-solving process. However, it is possible to make finer distinctions within some of the broad categories that Guideline 5.1 treats as equivalent. For example, the choice of a general-purpose search strategy also has implications for the expert system's ability to make good use of its resources. The Data-Driven Reasoning provided by Forward-Chaining Search allows the expert system to immediately recognize the implications of evidence that strongly suggests a particular hypothesis (Guideline 5.4). This rapid appreciation of the consequences of new information is important in some problems. In other problems, the Goal-Driven Reasoning provided by Backward-Chaining Search leads to a better expenditure of resources. This will be the case if it is important to be sure that all inferences made could help achieve the expert system's current goals.

5.1.1 Support for Example Guideline 5.1

The options that are available for choosing the next line of reasoning to pursue should be compared with the options that are available for choosing the next piece of information to gather, that is, Guideline 5.2.

Domain Knowledge Determines Next Task

Both CRYSALIS (first quote) and HASP/SIAP (second quote) use domain knowledge encoded in Control-Rules to order tasks.

> The method of interpreting protein EDM's [electron-density maps] is, at its critical points, opportunistic. Where to start, when to leave one part of the structure and focus upon another, what level of detail to look at, when to stop—these questions are continually presented to the expert as he builds his structure. The knowledge needed to answer them is almost entirely heuristic, and as subject to change as any other task-specific knowledge. It thus seems natural, and indeed has shown to be practical, that this strategic knowledge, which controls the order in which various tasks are performed, be represented as rules [Engelmore and Terry 1979, p. 255].

> The *knowledge of how to perform*, that is, how to use the available knowledge, is another kind of knowledge that the analysts possess. This type of knowledge is represented in the form of *control rules* to promote flexibility in specifying and modifying analysis strategies. [Nii, Feigenbaum, Anton, and Rockmore 1982].
> — Reprinted with permission from *AI Magazine*, 1982, p. 27, published by the American Association for Artificial Intelligence.

Costs and Benefits

Both quotes that follow argue for the use of intelligent schedulers when there are many possible lines of reasoning that could be explored. The first quote, which is from a description of the HEARSAY-II speech-understanding system, also mentions the need for Meta-Knowledge about the expected results of pursuing a line of reasoning. This Meta-Knowledge is provided by the response frame of a knowledge source.

> Because of the inherent uncertainty in the speech-understanding task, there are inevitably large numbers of plausible alternative actions in each time interval of the utterance. Before the correct interpretation has been found, we cannot evaluate with certainty the prospective value of any potential action.

The major impediment to discovery of the best overall interpretation in this scheme is the combinatorial explosion of KS [Knowledge Source] invocations that can occur. From the outset, numerous alternative actions are warranted. A purely top-down approach would generate a vast number of possible actions, if unrestrained. Because certainty of recognition is practically never possible and substantial numbers of competing hypotheses must be entertained at each time interval of analysis, any bottom-up approach generates a similarly huge number of competing possible actions. Thus additional constraints on the problem-solving activity must be enforced. This is accomplished by selecting for execution only a limited subset of the invoked KSs.

The objective of *selective attention* is to allocate limited computing resources (processing cycles) to the most important and most promising actions. This selectivity involves three components. First, the probable effects of a potential KS action must be estimated before it is performed. Second, the global significance of an isolated action must be deduced from analysis of its cooperative and competitive relationships with existing hypotheses; *globally significant actions* are those that contribute to the detection, formation, or extension of combinations of redundant hypotheses. Third, the desirability of an action must be assessed in comparison with other potential actions. While the inherent uncertainty of the speech task precludes error-free performance of these component tasks, there have been devised some approximate methods that effectively control the combinatorics and make the speech-understanding problem tractable.

Selective attention is accomplished in the Hearsay-II system by a heuristic scheduler which calculates a priority for each action and executes, at each time, the waiting action with the highest priority [Hayes-Roth and Lesser 1977]. The priority calculation attempts to estimate the usefulness of the action in fulfilling the overall system goal of recognizing the utterance. The calculation is based on information provided when the condition part of a KS is satisfied. This information includes the *stimulus frame*, which is the set of hypotheses that satisfied the condition, and the *response frame*, a stylized description of the blackboard modifications that the KS action is likely to perform. For example, consider a syllable-based word hypothesizer KS (such as MOW); its stimulus frame would include the specific syllable hypothesis which matched its condition, and its response frame would specify the expected action of generating word hypotheses in a time interval spanning that of the stimulus frame [Erman, Hayes-Roth, Lesser, and Reddy 1980, p. 221].

The AM system is a mathematics discovery system. It starts with knowledge of mathematical concepts about set theory, heuristics about how to develop new concepts, and heuristics about what kinds of new concepts are most interesting. Starting from this knowledge, AM managed to define many of the important concepts of elementary number theory (e.g., the concept of prime numbers) and formed the conjecture known as the *Fundamental Theorem of Arithmetic*.

A job-list scheme is a natural mechanism to use to manage the task-selection problem AM faces.

Recall that AM must zero in on one of the best few tasks to perform next, and it repeatedly makes this choice. At each moment, there might be thousands of directions to explore (plausible tasks to consider).

If all the legal tasks were written out, and reasons were thought up to support each one, then perhaps we could order them by the strength of those reasons, and thereby settle on the "best" task to work on next. In order to appear "smart" to the human user, AM should *never* execute a task having no reasons attached.

Some magical function exists, which provides a numeric rating, a priority value, for any given task. The function looks at a given facet/concept pair, examines all the associated reasons supporting that task, and computes an estimate of how worthwhile it would be for AM to spend some time now working on that facet of that concept.

So AM will maintain a list of those legal tasks which have some good reasons tacked onto them, which justify why each task should be executed, why it is plausible. At least implicitly, AM has a numeric rating for each task.

Give or take a few features, this notion of a "job-list" is the one which AM uses. It is also called an *agenda*[1] [Lenat 1976, pp. 32–33].
— Reprinted by permission of author.

5.2 Choice of Next Information to Request

Is it feasible to request all the available information that is relevant?

or

[1]Borrowed from Kaplan's term for the job-list present in KRL (see Bobrow and Winograd [1977]). For an earlier general discussion of agendas, see Knuth [1968].

Is it important to make the best use of the limited information that has been provided?

or

Is it necessary to weigh the potential benefits and costs of requesting particular items of information?

Evidence: Any   Type: Preenumerated, constructed

Request whatever data → *Goal-Driven Reasoning* (i.e., *Backward-*
are available   *Chaining* rule invocation)

More important to → *Data-Driven Reasoning* (i.e., *Forward-*
make the best use of   *Chaining* rule invocation)
limited data

Weigh benefits and → Choose questions according to the impact
costs   they are likely to have given the particular
   reasoning method in use {expensive}.

Goal-Driven Reasoning

MYCIN's built-in strategy is cautious: gather as much information as possible (without demanding new tests) for and against likely causes and then weigh the evidence. Operationally, this translates into exhaustive rule invocation whereby (a) all relevant rules are tried and (b) all rules whose left-hand sides match the case (and whose right-hand sides are relevant to problem-solving goals) have their right-hand sides acted upon. But under different circumstances, other strategies would be more appropriate. In emergencies, for example, physicians cannot take the time to gather much history data. Or, with recurring illness, physicians will order new tests and wait for the results. Deciding on the most appropriate strategy depends on medical knowledge about the context of the case. MYCIN's control structure is not concerned with resource allocation; it assumes that there is time to gather all available information that is relevant and time to process it. Thus MYCIN asks 20–70 questions and processes 1–25 rules between questions. We estimate that MYCIN executes about 50 rules per second (exclusive of I/O wait time). With larger amounts of data or larger numbers of rules, the control structure would need additional meta-rules that estimate the costs of gathering data and executing rules, in order to weigh costs against benefits. Also, in crisis situations or real-time data interpretation, the control structure would need to be concerned with the allocation of resources[2] [Buchanan and Shortliffe 1984, pp. 504f.].

Data-Driven Reasoning

The VM system monitors the status of patients attached to a mechanical ventilator that is providing breathing assistance. In this environment the system does not have the luxury of requesting whatever information it might find useful. Instead it must reason with whatever information is available.

The VM rule interpreter is based on the MYCIN interpreter. The major changes include (1) forward-chaining (data-driven) rule invocation as opposed to backward chaining, (2) checking to see that information acquired in a previous time frame is still valid for making conclusions, and (3) cycling through appropriate parts of the rule set each time new information is available.

A data-driven approach is necessary to take advantage of the small set of measurement values available in each time frame. This means that the reasoning process works forward from the available information as opposed to working backward from a goal and obtaining information as necessary. Because of the demanding nature of the ICU [Intensive Care Unit] environment, the system must acquire and interpret data with minimal staff intervention [Fagan, Shortliffe, and Buchanan 1984, p. 248].

Weigh Costs and Benefits

An accurate assessment of the benefits that would result from an answer to a question generally depends on the type of reasoning method used by the expert system and the details of the program's current hypotheses. The first of the following two quotes suggests how the evaluation of questions might be made for systems that follow a Group-

---

[2]In the AM and EURISKO programs [Lenat, 1976, 1983], Lenat has added information about maximum amounts of time to spend on various tasks, which keeps those programs from "overspending" computer time on difficult tasks of low importance. (EURISKO can also decide to change those time allocations.) In PROSPECTOR [Duda et al. 1978], attention is focused on the rules that will add the most information, i.e., that will most increase or decrease the probability of the hypothesis being pushed. In Fox's system [Fox 1981], the *estimated cost* of evaluating premises of rules helps determine what rules to invoke.

and-Differentiate strategy. The second quote describes the evaluation of questions for systems that rank hypotheses independently according to Scoring Functions. Slagle, Gaynor, and Halpern [1984] also evaluate questions according to their anticipated impact on Scoring Functions.

> This strategy as described has one failing: it assumes that all the evidence has already been gathered. In some domains (e.g., that of MYCIN), this is a reasonable assumption. In the domain of simple electronic reasoning, there are many tests that could be run. It would be silly to run them all before the consultation begins. Instead, the system doesn't run any until it is faced with a choice situation that requires more information to separate the two leading candidates. Then it runs whatever test seems most profitable, that is, the one that will apparently produce the biggest impact on the evidence totals for the leading candidates at the least cost [McDermott, D. and Brooks 1982].
> — Reprinted with permission from *Proceedings of the National Conference on Artificial Intelligence*, 1982, p. 371, published by the American Association for Artificial Intelligence.

Here are some of the intuitive considerations that are used by EXPERT and other systems to determine during a session whether one question is a better candidate than another.

1. Ask the least costly question. The question can be assigned cost or risk measures and the least costly questions ought to be asked before the more expensive questions. Since precise cost or risk in the literal sense is very difficult to assign, cost is usually taken to be an approximate ordering heuristic.

2. Give preference to those questions which affect the currently highest-weighted hypotheses. Select questions which appear in production rules which conclude those hypotheses with the highest current confidence.

3. Consider only those hypotheses which are related to a currently reported finding.

4. Consider only those findings which can potentially increase or decrease the current ranking of a hypothesis by some specified threshold.

5. Terminate questioning if the confidence in any hypothesis exceeds a predetermined threshold. This type of termination strategy is not used often, because one would usually want to ask more questions rather than stop early with a possible wrong answer. This is particularly true for a system which has sequential reasoning capabilities that immedi-

ately allow the user to see the current ranking of conclusions [Weiss and Kulikowski 1984, pp. 99f.].

5.3 Selectivity in Requesting Information

Should certain facts be established before the expert system requests a particular item of information (that item might be irrelevant, not crucial, or too expensive to attain)?

or

Would it be possible to ask for the same information for every problem?

Evidence: Any   Type: Any

Gathering information → Explicitly represent *Dependencies between*
in stages is important   *Hypotheses* and/or use *"Screening Clauses"*
in Rules.

Always the same set → *Questionnaire* {cheap}
of items

The first quote is taken from a description of PROSPECTOR, which is an expert system that aids geologists in the evaluation of exploration sites. The PROSPECTOR context mechanism makes it possible to ensure that no attempt will be made to establish a particular hypothesis until a specified degree of confidence has been reached in some other hypothesis. The second quote explains how the dependency information provided by a causal network enables the medical diagnosis system CADUCEUS to make conclusions based on easily accessible data before requesting data that are difficult to obtain.

It sometimes happens that assertions cannot be considered in an arbitrary order, but must be considered in a particular sequence. For example, one should determine that there is a relevant continental margin mobile belt before considering its age. This is more than a matter of preference since it would be meaningless for the program to ask about the age of a nonexistent belt.... In general, we use contexts to express a condition that must be established before an assertion can be used in the reasoning process [Duda, Gaschnig, and Hart 1979, p. 161].

> — Copyright 1979, Edinburgh University Press. Reprinted by permission.

The advantage of such a refined differential diagnosis is the opportunity it provides for establishing milestones in a diagnostic workup. The presence of pathological states represented by many of the nodes in the network can often be suggested and even confirmed on the basis of fairly commonplace clinical data. This is typically not true of the more remote (i.e., less observable) disease entities that inhabit the far reaches of the causal net, which often require for their confirmation some definitive, often costly procedure such as biopsy, arteriography, CAT scan evaluation, etc. [Pople 1982, pp. 153–154].

> — Pople, H. E., Jr. Heuristic methods for imposing structure on ill-structured problems: The structuring of medical diagnostics. In *Artificial Intelligence in Medicine*, P. Szolovits (ed). Boulder, CO: Westview Press, American Association for the Advancement of Science, 1982, pp. 119–190. Copyright 1982, American Association for the Advancement of Science. Reprinted by permission.

5.4 Speed of Response to Inputs

When evidence is available that strongly confirms or disconfirms a particular hypothesis, will it be important for the system to immediately recognize the implications of this evidence?

or

Will it be acceptable for the system to continue pursuing hypotheses in the order it had originally scheduled?

Evidence: Any   Type: Preenumerated, constructed

Immediately recognize → *Event-Driven Reasoning* (i.e., *Forward-*
the implications of   *Chaining*)
evidence

Pursue one hypothesis → *Goal-Driven Reasoning* (i.e., *Backward-*
at a time   *Chaining*)

[In Depth-First, Goal-Directed Search]...a startling piece of evidence (strongly suggesting a different hypothesis) *cannot* cause suspension of the current investigation and pursuit of the alternative [Smith and Clayton 1983, p. 155].

The main disadvantage of this control strategy [Goal-Directed Reasoning] is that users cannot interrupt to steer the line of reasoning by volunteering new information. A user can become frustrated, knowing that the system's present line of reasoning will turn out to be fruitless as a result of data that are going to be requested later [Buchanan and Shortliffe 1984, p. 678].

> — Buchanan/Shortliffe, *Rule-Based Expert Systems*, © 1984 by B. G. Buchanan and E. H. Shortliffe. Reprinted with permission of Addison-Wesley Publishing Co., Inc., Reading, Massachusetts.

5.5 *Aggressive or Conservative Search*

Does solving this problem require a search for solutions?

and

When considering the length of time it takes the system to find a solution: Is it better to sometimes produce an answer very fast, at the risk of having to wait a very long time on other occasions?

or

Is it better to give up the possibility of a very fast answer to protect against having to wait a very long time?

Evidence: Any   Type: Preenumerated, constructed

Sometimes produce a   → *Depth-First Search*
fast answer

Avoid a very slow   → *Breadth-First Search*
answer

Figure 5.1 illustrates the expected difference in the variance of solution times between Depth-First Search and Breadth-First Search. The histograms illustrate a hypothetical case where the average solution time is the same for the two search schemes, but Depth-First Search has

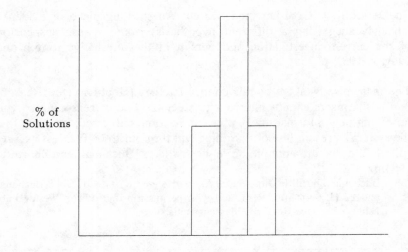

Breadth-First Search
Solution Time

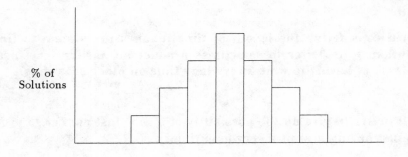

Depth-First Search
Solution Time

Figure 5.1. Breadth-First Search is more conservative than Depth-First Search. Breadth-First Search would be expected to have fewer very fast solutions and fewer very slow solutions.

more extreme values. The following quote describes how this difference in variance arises.

Warning: depth-first search is an aggressive but dangerous procedure.... A process doing depth-first movement through such a tree is likely to slip past the level at which the F node [the goal] appears and waste incredible energy exhaustively exploring parts of the tree lower down.... When depth-first search is a poor idea, breadth-first movement may be useful. Breadth-first searches look for the destination among all nodes at a given level before using the branches descending from those nodes to push on. ...Although the breadth-first search idea is careful and conservative, it can be wasteful. If all paths lead to the destination node at more or less the same depth, then breadth-first search works harder than depth-first search [Winston 1977, pp. 91–92].

The features designed into DENDRAL programs to make them easier and more pleasant to use include...depth-first problem solving to produce some solutions quickly, estimators of problem size and (at any time) amount of work remaining [Buchanan and Feigenbaum 1978, p. 316].

6 The Nature of Solutions

Knowledge engineers need to achieve a clear understanding about the circumstances that will entitle the expert system to stop and declare that the problem is solved. Different stopping criteria will be appropriate in different problem domains. For example, the output of the R1 expert system [McDermott, J. 1982] is a functionally acceptable VAX system configuration. There is no guarantee the optimal configuration is found, but R1 is quite useful nonetheless. In other problem domains an expert system would need to keep working until an optimal solution is found.

A closely related question concerns the number of solutions that are expected. Some medical expert systems can safely assume patients will only have one of the diseases the expert system is capable of diagnosing, for example, the expert system discussed in Reggia, Nau, and Wang [1984], for determining the cause of the wasting of the muscles of the lower legs. Other medical expert systems must be prepared to deal with patients with multiple diseases. The following guideline makes recommendations for the case where it is not reasonable to stop the diagnostic process as soon as one solution is found.

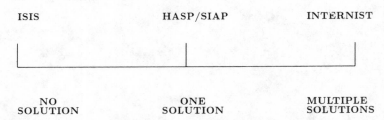

Figure 6.1. Expert-system problems can be distinguished by the number of solutions that are expected. The three expert systems shown differ in the number of solutions they are prepared to handle. The ISIS system is an expert system that can cope with the possibility that there is no solution to the problem as originally stated.

6.1 Multiple Faults

Is this a diagnosis problem?

and

Would it be unwise to assume that there is only a single underlying fault because multiple faults are either too common or too serious to run the risk of a misdiagnosis?

Evidence: Any   Type: Any

Yes → Solve a sequence of problems that "subtract off" previously accounted for manifestations. The system will need to use heuristic criteria to determine the most parsimonious explanation and also to distinguish between competing and complementary hypotheses.

Discussions of the subtractive method recommended in Guideline 6.1 and examples of heuristics for judging parsimony and detecting competitors can be found in Pople [1977, p. 1032]; Reggia, Nau, and Wang [1983, 1984]; Patil [1981]; and Patil, Szolovits and Schwartz [1981].

As Figure 6.1 suggests, there is a continuum of expert-system problems ranging from multiple solutions at one extreme, passing through a point where there is exactly one legitimate solution, and finally reaching a point at the other extreme where there are no solutions to the problem as originally stated. The diagnosis of multiple diseases by the INTERNIST [Pople 1977] expert system provides an example of the "multiple solutions" point on this continuum. The ISIS system [Fox 1983] provides an example of the "no solutions" point on this continuum in its attempts to construct job-shop schedules that satisfy a number of constraints. It often turns out that there are implicit conflicts between the constraints making it impossible to find any schedule that satisfies them all. The ISIS system employs a constraint relaxation scheme to define new problems that have a better chance of being successfully solved. This issue is discussed in Guideline 6.6.

Sensor interpretation problems will often be examples of the "one solution" point on this continuum. If we can assume that there is some true state of the world that gives rise to the sensor data, then, in principle, there is only one legitimate solution. If the sensor data are sufficiently rich to uniquely determine the underlying state of the world, then an interpretation expert system can be satisfied with finding one solution [Feigenbaum 1977, p. 1025]. This issue is discussed in Guideline 6.3.

6.1.1 Support for Example Guideline 6.1

Subtractive Method

In discussing the strategy of problem formulation in INTERNIST-1, it is important that we have a clearly defined interpretation of what is meant by the terms used. The term "problem" is taken to mean a collection of disease entities, one and only one of which is considered possible in the case being analyzed. ...In many computer-based diagnostic systems, the problem (so-defined) is pre-determined and the program's job is simply to select one of a fixed list of disease entities that best fits the facts of a case. In cases where more than one disease may be present, however, it is necessary to partition the set of disease entities evoked by a given set of observed manifestations into disjoint subsets, each of which meets the "problem" specification given above.

Whenever a problem becomes solved; it is entered into a list of concluded diagnoses; all manifestations explained by that disease are marked "accounted for"; and the process recycles until all problems present in the case have been uncovered [p. 1032].
 — Pople, H. E., Jr. The formation of composite hypotheses in diagnostic problem solving: An exercise in synthetic reasoning. *Proceedings of the Fifth International Joint Conference on Artificial Intelligence*, Cambridge, MA, 1977, pp. 1030–1037. Used by permission of the International Joint

Conferences on Artificial Intelligence, Inc.; copies of this and other IJ-CAI Proceedings are available from Morgan Kaufmann Publishers, Inc., PO Box 50490, Palo Alto, CA 94303, USA.

When it makes sense to view a fault as causing a portion of a symptom, then instead of subtracting off an entire symptom as accounted for, it is better to subtract off just the portion of a symptom that can be attributed to the concluded fault.

One of the important areas of medical diagnosis not adequately addressed by the first generation of AIM [Artificial Intelligence in Medicine] programs is the evaluation of the effect of more than one disease present in the patient simultaneously, especially when one of the diseases alters the presentation of the others. For example, let us consider a patient with diarrhea and vomiting leading to severe hypokalemia. Let us also suppose that we know about the diarrhea, but we are not aware of the vomiting. The observed hypokalemia is too severe to be properly accounted for by the diarrhea alone and therefore diarrhea cannot be considered as a complete explanation for the observed hypokalemia. Given this fact, the diarrhea is either not responsible for hypokalemia or is only partly responsible. If the diarrhea is not responsible, then further reasoning is relatively easy: the problem simplifies to finding the actual cause. However, if diarrhea is partly responsible, a correct partitioning of the total observed hypokalemia between two suspected causes is required, with a judgment of how well the two separate causes combined in the estimated proportions account for the patient's condition.[1] Notice how inadequate the simple assigning of a probability linking diarrhea and hypokalemia (as is commonly done in existing programs) is to capture the problem being described here [p. 10].

One of the important mechanisms in developing an understanding of the patient's illness is the evaluation of the effects of more than one disease present in the patient simultaneously, especially when one of the diseases alters the presentation of the others. To deal with such a situation competently, the program must have the ability to identify the effect of each cause individually, and the ability to combine these effects together. ...Component summation combines attributes of the components to generate the attributes of the joint node; component decomposition identifies the unaccounted component by noting differences between the joint node and its existing components. These operations enrich the PSM [Patient-Specific Model] by instantiating and unifying component nodes

---

[1]All the previous programs allow the entire hypokalemia to be accounted for by diarrhea. In particular, INTERNIST-1 after allowing the hypokalemia to be accounted for by diarrhea, will not allow hypokalemia to lend any support to the hypothesis of vomiting. PIP, on the other hand, will allow the entire hypokalemia to lend support to the hypothesis of vomiting as well as allowing it to be explained by diarrhea.

when the case demands them. This occurs whenever multiple causes contribute jointly to a single effect. An important case of this arises whenever feedback is modeled, because in any feedback loop there is at least one node acted on both by an outside factor and by the feedback loop itself. Finally, the decomposition of an effect with multiple causes into its causal components will also provide us with valuable information for evaluating the prognosis and formulating therapeutic interventions [p. 72] [Patil 1981].

Competing versus Complementary Hypotheses

The following quote describes the INTERNIST-1 heuristic for deciding whether two hypotheses are competing explanations so that only one of them should be included in the final answer. Reggia, Nau, and Wang [1983, p. 336] have argued that this heuristic will sometimes fail to correctly identify competitors.

Given a ranked list of disease hypotheses, a problem is then formulated on the basis of the most highly rated of these items, using the following heuristic criterion: two disease entities are considered to be alternatives to one another [that is, competitors] ... if, taken together, they explain no more of the observed findings than are explained by one or the other separately [p. 1032].

— Pople, H. E., Jr. The formation of composite hypotheses in diagnostic problem solving: An exercise in synthetic reasoning. *Proceedings of the Fifth International Joint Conference on Artificial Intelligence*, Cambridge, MA, 1977, pp. 1030–1037. Used by permission of the International Joint Conferences on Artificial Intelligence, Inc.; copies of this and other IJCAI Proceedings are available from Morgan Kaufmann Publishers, Inc., PO Box 50490, Palo Alto, CA 94303, USA.

We propose the use of a *coherent hypothesis* as the logical unit of hypothesis representation. This captures our notion ... that the reasoner's hypothesis structure must account for the total state of mind of the reasoner including its current uncertainties. In the program, each coherent hypothesis is represented using a *patient specific model* (PSM). Each PSM represents a causal explanation of all the observed findings and their interrelationships at various levels of detail. Note that within each PSM all the diseases, findings, etc., are mutually complementary, while the alternate PSM's are mutually exclusive and competing [Patil 1981, pp. 27–28].

6.2 Novel Faults or Predictable Faults

If the expert system will be solving a diagnosis problem, then will it be necessary to diagnose novel faults that the human experts have never seen before?

or

Are the faults of interest limited and predictable?

Evidence: Any   Type: Any

Novel faults   → *"Deep" Reasoning*; also called *Causal Models* and *Reasoning from First Principles* {expensive}.

Type: Constructed, simulation

Predictable faults   → *"Shallow" Reasoning*; also called *Heuristic Classification* and *Compiled Evidence*—usually implemented with *Rules*.

Type: Preenumerated

Deep Reasoning

In the following quote Randall Davis contrasts systems that Reason from First Principles with rule-based systems that capture an expert's response to previous problems.

> Finally, reasoning from first principles offers the possibility of dealing with novel faults. As we have seen, our system does not depend for its performance on a catalog of observed error manifestations. Instead it takes the view that any discrepancy between observed and expected behavior is a bug, and it uses knowledge about the device structure and behavior to determine the possible sources of the bug. As a result, it is able to reason about bugs that are novel in the sense that they are not part of the "training set" and are manifested by symptoms not seen previously.

Since rules are a distillation of an expert's experience, a program built from them will be reasonably sure of handling only cases quite similar to those the human expert has already seen, solved, and communicated to the program. We have little reason to believe that the program will handle a bug whose outward manifestation is unfamiliar, even if the root cause is within the claimed scope of the system [p. 391].

> — Davis, R. Diagnostic reasoning based on structure and behavior. *Artificial Intelligence*, *24*, 347–410 (1984). Copyright 1984, Elsevier Science Publishers B.V.

Shallow Reasoning

In the following quote Gary Kahn argues that while a diagnostic expert system that takes a dynamic approach, (i.e., that manipulates a causal model) has the capability of dealing with novel problems, that capability is not important for the oil-well drilling fluids domain of the MUD system.

What one may lose in not taking a **dynamic** approach is the ability to come up with novel hypotheses. This loss, however, is not significant where the range of expected problems and contexts of use are limited and predictable. In the mud domain [that is, oil-well drilling fluids] the range of expected problems is small. That is, there are about about 10 typically used muds, whose behavior under various conditions is well understood. There are probably only on the order of a dozen subsurface events which are of diagnostic interest. Some additional problems are caused by overtreatments and undertreatments with chemical additives. There are probably fewer than a dozen treatment additives that may be misused in such a way as to create problems for any particular type of mud [p. 26].

> — Kahn, G. On when diagnostic systems want to do without causal knowledge. In *ECAI-84: Advances in Artificial Intelligence*, T. O'Shea (ed.), Amsterdam: Elsevier, 1984, pp. 21–30. Copyright 1984, Elsevier Science Publishers B.V.

6.3 Single Hypothesis or Multiple Hypotheses

Are there a series of data-gathering opportunities for each problem?

and

Is there a single solution that remains the same, or changes only slightly, between data-gathering opportunities?

and

Are the data that are available for a problem generally sufficient to uniquely determine the correct solution?

Evidence: Any   Type: Any

Yes → Maintain only a single, "best" hypothesis between data-gathering sessions.

Evidence: Moderate, powerful

No → Maintain several, candidate hypotheses.

The HASP/SIAP expert system interprets data from underwater acoustic sensors to determine ship positions. As discussed in the following quote, for this problem it was necessary to keep only a single, best hypothesis. Speech understanding, by contrast, is a domain where it might be preferable to maintain several, candidate hypotheses.

> The system [HASP/SIAP] uses the simplifying strategy of maintaining only one "best" situation-hypothesis at any moment, modifying it incrementally as required by the changing data. This approach is made feasible by several characteristics of the domain. First, there is the strong continuity over time of objects and their behaviors (specifically, they do not change radically over time, or behave radically different over short periods). Second, a single problem (identity, location and velocity of a particular set of objects) persists over numerous data gathering periods. (Compare this to speech understanding in which each sentence is spoken just once, and each presents a new and different problem.) Finally, the system's hypothesis is typically "almost right," in part because it gets numerous opportunities to refine the solution (i.e., the numerous data gathering periods), and in part because the availability of many knowledge sources tends to over-determine the solution. As a result of all these, the current best hypothesis changes only slowly with time, and hence keeping only the current best is a feasible approach [Feigenbaum 1977, p. 1025].
> — © 1977 Edward A. Feigenbaum

There is also an alternative point of view that argues that an expert system should never be designed to maintain only a single, best hypothesis. According to this view, an expert system should always allow for the possibility that it will not be able to choose between several different hypotheses. Given any particular set of mechanisms for resolving conflict between competing hypotheses, there will be times when those mechanisms successfully resolve the conflict leaving only one remaining candidate, and other times when those mechanisms cannot resolve the conflict and several equally plausible candidates remain. In either case, if the expert system is designed to maintain more than one candidate hypothesis, then it will not be put in the position of having to make an arbitrary decision about which candidate to maintain.

6.4 Preenumerated or Constructed Solutions

Can all the possible solutions that the expert system needs to consider be listed in advance?

and

Is there heuristic knowledge available that tells us what sorts of findings implicate each of these solutions?

Evidence: Any   Type: Any

Preenumerated
solutions
→ Use *Rules* to encode the heuristic knowledge—that is, *Heuristic Association.* Simple data structures such as *Variables*, *Assertions*, or *Attribute–Object–Value Triples* may be sufficient for knowledge representation {cheap}.

Constructed solutions
→ Use more elaborate data structures and inference processes to support the assembly, modification, and refinement of tentative solutions.

To *select* a solution, the problem solver needs experiential ("expert") knowledge in the form of *patterns of problems and solutions* and heuristics relating them. To *construct* a solution, the problem solver applies models of structure and behavior, in the form of constraints and inference operators, by which objects can be designed, assembled, diagnosed, employed in some plan, etc. [p. 344].

The essential differences between heuristic construction and classification are the need for some "data structure" to post the assembled solution and operators for proposing and reasoning about solution fragments [Erman, London, and Fickas 1981] [p. 334] [Clancey 1985].

The EXPERT system is a shell for building heuristic classification systems that represents findings and hypotheses such as "the color of the car is green" with a single variable, say, CRGRN, that can take on the values true, false, or unavailable. Simple as it is, this knowledge representation format has been capable of supporting a number of classification expert systems that perform at high levels.

The alternative approach used by other systems, such as EMYCIN or PROSPECTOR is to describe hypotheses or findings as triples of object, attribute, value. An example of such a triple would be "the color of the car is green." In this example the object is the car, the attribute (or logically speaking the predicate) is color, and the value is green. While these triples are somewhat richer in structure than the simple findings and hypotheses that we will use in our examples, either approach may often be used for classification systems. In logical terms, EXPERT works mostly at the simpler propositional logic level, whereas EMYCIN and PROSPECTOR include many expressions of the predicate (functional) logic level [Weiss and Kulikowski 1984, p. 81].
  — Copyright 1984, Sholom M. Weiss and Casimir A. Kulikowski. Reprinted by permission.

The following quote compares GENEX and GENEX II, two expert systems that employ different approaches to solving the same class of problems from genetics. GENEX operates with a preenumerated set of solutions described in terms of "large-grained empirical [i.e., heuristic] knowledge." By contrast, the fine-grained knowledge that GENEX II requires to construct new solutions leads to longer chains of inference than used in GENEX.

I constructed two programs that solve problems in the same domain, with the same objectives, but each using a different reasoning method. GENEX [Koton 1983] and GENEX II [Koton 1985a] solve problems about the behavior of bacterial operons, a subfield of molecular biology. Both take as input a description of an operon (real or imaginery) and information on whether or not the genes of that operon are expressed, then attempt to deduce the biological control mechanism causing the observed behavior of the operon. GENEX uses large-grained empirical knowledge to solve problems, and GENEX II uses model-based reasoning. GENEX II can solve a greater variety of problems and more difficult problems than GENEX [p. 297].

For small domains, it may be possible to enumerate every possible situation and encode a response for each one. In a large domain, it may be extremely difficult to predict every possible state of the system. In contrast, a system which uses model-based reasoning, such as GENEX II, can *generate* new situations based on its underlying model of the domain [p. 298f.].

As always, there are tradeoffs. Model-based systems such as GENEX II require a more complicated control structure to reduce the amount of search for possible solutions. The fine-grained knowledge in GENEX II creates inference chains that are about four times longer than those generated by GENEX in the solution of the same problem. This results in a slower-executing program. Perhaps the ideal system would use both empirical associations for speed and model-based reasoning for improved problem-solving ability and better understanding of its reasoning, as described by [Barnett, 1982] [p. 299] [Koton 1985b].

> — Koton, P. A. Empirical and model-based reasoning in expert systems. *Proceedings of the Ninth International Joint Conference on Artificial Intelligence*, 1985, pp. 297–299. Used by permission of the International Joint Conferences on Artificial Intelligence, Inc.; copies of this and other IJCAI Proceedings are available from Morgan Kaufmann Publishers, Inc., PO Box 50490, Palo Alto, CA 94303, USA.

6.5 First Solution or All Solutions

Are all plausible solutions required? (Perhaps because overlooking a possible solution or accepting a less than optimal solution leads to costly or dangerous situations.)

or

Is just one solution required?

Evidence: Any   Type: Any

All solutions   → *Exhaustive Search {expensive}* or *Generate-and-Test*

Heuristic DENDRAL is organized as a Plan–Generate–Test sequence. This is not necessarily the same method used by chemists, but is easily understood by them. It complements their methods by providing such a meticulous search through the space of molecular structures that the chemist is virtually guaranteed that any candidate structure which fails to appear on the final list of plausible structures has been rejected for explicitly stated chemical reasons [Buchanan and Feigenbaum 1978, p. 8].

In many data-analysis tasks it is desirable to find every interpretation that is consistent with the data. This conservative attitude is standard in high-risk applications, such as the analysis of poisonous substances or medical diagnosis. A systematic approach would be to consider all possible cases and to rule out those inconsistent with the data. ...The DENDRAL program (Buchanan and Feigenbaum 1978) is probably the best known program that reasons by elimination (using generate-and-test) [p. 149].

— Stefik, M., Aikins, J., Balzer, R., Benoit, J., Birnbaum, L., Hayes-Roth, F., and Sacerdoti, E. The organization of expert systems, a tutorial. *Artificial Intelligence*, *18*, 135–173 (1982). Copyright 1982, Elsevier Science Publishers B.V.

6.6 Relationship between Objectives

The following guideline asks whether there is potential conflict between the separate objectives for a task. One example of such conflict arises in machining parts where producing one of the desired holes or slots might destroy the clamping surfaces needed to produce another desired hole or slot [Hayes 1987].

Is the expert system trying to achieve several different objectives in a construction, arrangement, or design task? If so, what is the nature of the relationship between the various objectives?

1. **Independent objectives**

2. **Potentially conflicting objectives**

3. **Mutually supporting objectives**

4. **Loosely coupled objectives and satisfactory, but not necessarily optimal, solution required**

5. **Highly interlocked objectives or optimal solution required**

Evidence: Any   Type: Constructed

| Independent objectives | → | *Divide-and-Conquer* |

Independent objectives → *Divide-and-Conquer*

Conflicting objectives → *Constraint Relaxation* or *Maximize Utility Functions*

Mutually supporting objectives → *Prerequisites First* or *More General Objectives First*

Loosely coupled objectives and satisfactory, but not necessarily optimal, solution required → See Guideline 6.7

Highly interlocked objectives or optimal solution required → *Search*

Independent Objectives

Many AI programs have the ability to break a problem into subproblems, that is, to find a solution by a *divide and conquer* strategy.

When subproblems in a problem do not interact, they can be solved independently. However, the experience with problem-solving programs in the past few years has shown that this ideal situation is unusual in real world problems. Interactions appear even in highly simplified AI domains such as the blocks world [pp. 132f.].

    — Stefik, M. Planning with constraints (MOLGEN: Part 1). *Artificial Intelligence*, 16, 111–139 (1981a). Copyright 1981, Elsevier Science Publishers B.V.

Mutually Supporting or Potentially Conflicting Objectives

Given two goals, various relationships between them are possible:

- *Independence:* The goals do not affect each other.

- *Cooperation:* Achieving one goal makes it easier to achieve the other.

- *Competition:* One goal can be achieved only at the expense of the other.

- *Interference:* One goal must be achieved in a way that takes the other goal into account.

Independent goals can be achieved in any order, with the same net result. Thus no special control strategy is needed to order them; this decision can be made arbitrarily, or based on other factors; *e.g.*, relationships to other goals.

Cooperative goals [that is, Mutually Supporting Objectives] should be achieved in whichever order best exploits the relationship among them:

- *Achieve prerequisite first:* If one goal satisfies a precondition for achieving the other, achieving it first may generate information (*e.g.*, variable bindings) needed to solve the second goal.

- *Achieve more general goal first:* If one goal subsumes the other, achieving it first satisfies the less general goal without any additional work. This usually makes more sense than solving the simpler goal first and then trying to extend the solution to cover the more general case—but not always.

- *Learn by solving easier goal first:* If two goals are similar but one is harder, solving the easier goal first may serve as a way to generate additional knowledge useful in solving the harder goal. This strategy can be effective if the designer is capable of learning from experience.

Competitive goals [that is, Potentially Conflicting Objectives] must be integrated according to their relative importance:

- *Sacrifice less important goal:* If one goal completely dominates the other, ignore the less important goal.

- *Relax goal:* If both goals are important, relax one of them to a version that is weaker than the original but compatible with the other.

- *Treat as trade-off:* If the goals are relative preferences rather than absolute predicates, treat the competitive relationship (*e.g.*, between time-efficiency and space-efficiency) as a tradeoff, and choose a compromise solution to optimize (or satisfice) some overall utility function (*e.g.*, minimize a weighted sum of time and space).

[Mostow 1985].
— Reprinted with permission from *AI Magazine*, 1985, pp. 49f., published by the American Association for Artificial Intelligence.

Potentially Conflicting Objectives

The reaction of planning-constraint systems to conflicting constraints is to either look for a different plan, query the user for alterations, or end processing. In the CONSTRAINTS [Steele 1980] system for circuit analysis, conflict resulted in a null value set. The system would determine what assumptions are in conflict and ask the user to resolve them. In MOLGEN [Stefik 1981a], an alternative plan is searched for when value constraints cannot be satisfied. In these two systems, the constraints are either satisfied, or they are not satisfied, there is no middle ground.

In the scheduling domain there is a middle ground. As the NUDGE system [Goldstein and Roberts 1977] showed, constraints can be preferentially ordered. In job-shop scheduling, due dates can be missed by small amounts, more labor hired in overtime if there are not enough machine operators, orders sub-contracted, costs increased or reduced, etc. That is, constraints can be relaxed from their original definition. Consider the specification of a due-date constraint. While meeting the due date is important, shipping a bit early or a bit late is also ok, but being too late (tardy) or too early is not reasonable.

Our research will explore the representation of relaxation constraints and how to use them to resolve conflicts [Fox and Smith 1983, pp. 4f.].
— Reprinted by permission of author.

Because it is generally not possible to simultaneously satisfy all of constraints 1 through 6 below, the R1 system that constructs VAX configurations employs a relaxation scheme to find the best available configuration for unibus modules.

There are a number of independent constraints on the placing of unibus modules:

(1) Each module must be put in a backplane slot of the appropriate pinning type.

(2) The position of each backplane in a box must be such that its modules draw power from a single set of regulators.

(3) There is a limit on the amount of power that the modules in a backplane can collectively draw from any regulator.

(4) If a module requires panel space, that panel space must be in the cabinet containing the module.

(5) If a module requires other supporting modules either in the same backplane or in the same box, space must be available for those supporting modules.

(6) The modules should be placed on the unibus in a sequence that is as close to the optimal sequence as possible. [The optimal sequence is one in which the modules are ordered by their interrupt priority, and within a fixed level of interrupt priority they are ordered on the basis of their transfer rate].

If only the first five constraints applied, R1 would generate only acceptable unibus module configurations; but the addition of the sixth constraint, since it is elastic, makes that impossible. In order to limit the amount of search it has to do to configure the unibus modules, R1 interprets the sixth constraint somewhat liberally. It defines three equivalence classes of sequences: optimal (any ordering that is optimal), almost-optimal (any less than optimal ordering such that no module whose interrupt priority is i and whose transfer rate is j, occurs before a module whose interrupt priority is i and whose transfer rate is less than j), and suboptimal (any other ordering).

To configure a set of unibus modules, R1 first estimates the amount of space required to place the unibus modules optimally and the amount of space required to place the modules suboptimally; it then determines the optimal sequence. If the amount of box space available is greater than or equal to the space required for an optimal configuration, it tries to place the modules on the unibus in that sequence. If it fails (or if the amount of box space available is less than the space required for an optimal configuration, but greater than that required for a suboptimal configuration), it retries the subtask, modifying the sequence whenever such a modification would save space and results in an almost-optimal sequence. If this attempt fails, it retries the subtask again, but this time modifies the sequence whenever such a modification would save space. If this attempt fails or if the amount of box space available is less than that required for a suboptimal configuration, R1 adds another box to the order and tries again [pp. 51f.].

— McDermott, J. R1: A rule-based configurer of computer systems. *Artificial Intelligence*, *19*, 39–88 (1982). Copyright 1982, Elsevier Science Publishers B.V.

Highly Interlocking Objectives

NP-complete problems [see Horowitz and Sahni 1978] such as bin packing resist a decomposition into loosely coupled subproblems. The interdependencies are so thoroughly entwined that an acceptable decision about one component can be made confidently only after all the other components are in place. But that implies that there is no way to be equally confident about the decisions made about previously placed components.

> Given a limited amount of box space, the information that is needed to determine whether a module has been configured acceptably is not available until after all of the modules have been placed on the unibuses [p. 51].

> As the bin-packing (i.e., the unibus module placement) subtask shows, it depends in part on the specific nature of the task environment (i.e., whether its structure is sufficiently interlocking). Bin packing has been studied enough to attribute the necessity of search to the structure of the task [p. 56].
> — McDermott, J. R1: A rule-based configurer of computer systems. *Artificial Intelligence, 19*, 39–88 (1982). Copyright 1982, Elsevier Science Publishers B.V.

6.7 Achieving Interacting Goals

Is the expert system trying to achieve several different objectives in a construction, arrangement, or design task?

and

Are there relatively weak interactions between the objectives so that a solution to one of the objectives can generally be combined somehow with the solution to another objective? (That is: *The interactions between objectives do not totally dominate the solution process.*)

and

Is there no necessity for an optimal solution—just a satisfactory solution?

Then which of the following best describes the nature of the problem?

1. **At program-design time it will be possible to specify the prerequisite information that will allow each decision to be made with complete certainty.**

2. **The decisions that are most critical (i.e., most constraining) can be anticipated at program-design time.**

3. **At problem-solution time an examination of the detailed features of the current solution state is generally sufficient to provide compelling reasons in favor of some decision or other.**

4. **Satisfying an objective is a matter of degree so that it is natural to assess the extent to which a potential choice satisfies a particular objective.**

Evidence: Any   Type: Constructed

Anticipate prerequisites   → Order decisions so that all of the prerequisites required to make decisions with certainty are established; that is, *Match*.

Evidence: Weak, moderate

Anticipate criticality   → Order decisions so that the most critical decisions are made first; that is, *Top–Down Refinement*.

Constraints arise dynamically from problem characteristics   → Develop a language for describing solution characteristics that allows the expert system to commit itself to just those aspects of the solution it is certain about. *Nonlinear Plans* and *Least Commitment* are two examples of this strategy.

Evidence: Weak, moderate

Assign preferences to choices   → *Heuristic Search*, where the evaluation function is made sensitive to the interactions between objectives either by mathematically *Combining Preference Orderings* for different objectives or by using the preferences from one objective to *Break Ties* in the preferences of another objective.

When all else fails   → *Blind Search*

Blind Search

When solutions are constructed, instead of merely selected from a fixed set of possibilities, there are often too many possible combinations of components to make it feasible to use Blind Search methods (e.g., Forward-Chaining or Backward-Chaining) to find a satisfactory solution. These general-purpose search methods may be too inefficient in the face of the combinatorial explosion of possibilities that often arise in construction problems.

A capsule summary of the advantages and disadvantages of Blind Search as a method of solving problems that require constructing solutions is as follows:

> **Blind Search**
> - Universally applicable
> - Implementation: *easy*
> - Computational efficiency: *poor*

One way to improve the efficiency of search is to use heuristic evaluation functions that provide some information about when the search is on the right track. The use of this kind of heuristic search to deal with interacting objectives will be briefly discussed in the final supporting quote for this guideline.

The other techniques recommended in this guideline all attempt to use knowledge to achieve certainty in their decisions. By achieving certainty, these techniques avoid the necessity of searching and backtracking. These techniques all break down under some circumstances, and in these cases they are forced to fall back on search to continue to make progress.

Match

There are two steps involved in Match. The following quote discusses the first step, which is to specify the prerequisites that would allow each decision to be made with certainty.

When Match can be used to solve a problem, a path from the initial state to a solution state can be found without any backtracking. It follows that for Match to be applicable, it must be possible to order the set of relevant decisions in such a way that no decision has to be made until the information sufficient for making it is available. It should be clear that for complex problems (in which much of the information required at any decision point will be available only after other decisions are made) the applicability of Match rests entirely on whether it is possible to specify at each step what information is sufficient for that step. For most of the VAX-11 configuration task, it is possible to provide such a specification.

R1 implements Match by requiring that the conditions of each of its rules specify the conditions under which that rule can be safely applied; that is, no rule can be applied in a particular situation (or a particular state) unless all the information needed to insure that it will extend the configuration in an acceptable way is present. A typical rule is satisfied if (1) an unconfigured component with a particular set of characteristics is in working memory, and (2) descriptions of partial configurations and/or other unconfigured components with particular characteristics are in working memory. When the rule is applied, it specifies how that unconfigured component is to be associated with one or more of the other components [p. 825].

— McDermott, J., and Steele, B. Extending a knowledge-based system to deal with ad hoc constraints. *Proceedings of the Seventh International Joint Conference on Artificial Intelligence*, 1981, Vancouver, BC, pp. 824–828. Used by permission of the International Joint Conferences on Artificial Intelligence, Inc.; copies of this and other IJCAI Proceedings are available from Morgan Kaufmann Publishers, Inc., PO Box 50490, Palo Alto, CA 94303, USA.

A problem with the strategy of achieving certainty by specifying prerequisites in this "piecewise" fashion is that the lack of overall coordination can result in deadlock conditions. For example, an operator for choosing component B can specify that A is a prerequisite:

If A is known, then choose B (with complete certainty).

There is a potential deadlock if the operator for choosing A is

If B is known, then choose A (with complete certainty).

A good global organizer for producing the required coordination is a sequence of states. As described in the following quote, the operators can then simply check that the appropriate state has been achieved without checking each prerequisite individually. The following quote also makes the point that Match is not appropriate when an optimal solution is required instead of just a satisfactory solution.

Because Match is a powerful method, it should be considered for all tasks that can support its use. In order to support Match, a task must be decomposable; it must involve moving from an initial state, through a number of intermediate states, to some desired state. If there are several alternative desired states, they must be equally acceptable. It must be possible, at any intermediate state, to determine whether that state is on a solution path; this implies that whatever information is required in order to determine whether a state is on a solution path can be available when it is needed. Even if a task does not meet these requirements, Match may be able to be used in conjunction with other, less powerful, methods. In the configuration task, the desired states (acceptable configurations) are not all equally acceptable since unibus modules can be configured more or less optimally. Nevertheless, Match can be used as a stand-alone method to configure everything except unibus modules and as an embedded method to generate candidate unibus module sequences.

The fact that Match can be used for some task does not imply that its use is warranted. Match may be useable, but impractical. How practical Match is depends, at least in part, on how difficult it is to order the intermediate states in such a way that no state can be reached before all of the information required to determine if that state is on a solution path has become available. In task domains with little structure, this ordering may be almost impossible to achieve since each state would have to test explicitly for the availability of that information. In task domains with considerable structure, on the other hand, the ordering may be quite easy to achieve since the fact that some other state or set of states have already been visited may guarantee the availability of much of that information and thus only a few explicit tests would be required [p. 70f.].
— McDermott, J. R1: A rule-based configurer of computer systems. *Artificial Intelligence*, *19*, 39–88 (1982). Copyright 1982, Elsevier Science Publishers B.V.

A capsule summary of the advantages and disadvantages of Match as a way of avoiding search by achieving certainty is as follows:

Match—R1 [McDermott, J. 1982]
- The programmer must discover an ordering of states that achieves all prerequisites: *hard*
- Implementation: *easy*
- Computational efficiency: *good*
- Forced to search: *when optimal solution required*

Top–Down Refinement

Breaking up the construction of a plan into successive planning problems that deal with increasing detail permits the planning process to achieve certainty in two different ways:

1. The detailed levels of the plan are attempted only once a successful plan has been achieved at the higher levels of abstraction. Thus there is reasonable certainty that these details will actually contribute to a successful plan and time is not wasted searching for a way to achieve the details of a plan that is doomed to failure.
2. A set of objectives is considered to be a detail only if there appears to be a "short plan" that will achieve that objective whenever all the more critical objectives have been achieved (see Sacerdoti [1974, p. 120]). Thus because of the way details are defined, there is also high certainty that the detailed objectives can, in fact, be achieved.

A superior approach to problem solving would be to search first through an *abstraction space*, a simplifying representation of the problem space in which unimportant details are ignored. When a solution to the problem in the abstraction space is discovered, all that remains is to account for the details of the linkup between the steps of the solution. This can be regarded as a sequence of subproblems in the original problem space. If they can be solved, a solution to the overall problem will have been achieved. If they cannot be solved, more planning in the abstraction space is required to discover an alternative solution [p. 117].

This search strategy might be termed a "length-first" search. It pushes the planning process in each abstraction space all the way to the original goal state before beginning to plan in a lower space. This enables the system to recognize as early as possible the steps that would lead to dead ends or very inefficient plans [p. 121].

In summary, hierarchical planning using abstraction spaces in a "length-first" search technique postpones extending the search tree through the levels concerned with the detailed preconditions of an operator until it knows that doing so will be highly effectual in reaching the goal (because the operator lies along an almost certainly successful path). By avoiding work on fruitless branches of the search tree, the technique achieves significant efficiencies in the formulation of complex plans [p. 123].

— Sacerdoti, E. D. Planning in a hierarchy of abstraction spaces. *Artificial Intelligence, 5*, 115–135 (1974). Copyright 1974, Elsevier Science Publishers B.V.

A capsule summary of the advantages and disadvantages of Top–Down Refinement as a way of avoiding search is as follows:

> **Top–Down Refinement—ABSTRIPS [Sacerdoti 1974]**
> - Have to identify most critical choices: *moderate difficulty*
> - Implementation: *easy*
> - Computational efficiency: *good*
> - Forced to search: *within each criticality level*

Develop a Language in Order to Make the Least Commitment

The MOLGEN expert system uses Least Commitment and Constraint Posting to take advantage of constraints that arise in the solution of a particular problem. Each dynamically defined constraint can be posted with certainty as long as the constraint language is rich enough to allow the expert system to commit itself only to the extent that it is certain. The conjunction of all of these dynamically defined constraints is expected to provide compelling reasons for all of the choices that are required to construct a complete solution.

> In summary, the least-commitment principle coordinates decision-making with the availability of information and moves the focus of problem-solving activity among the various subproblems. The least-commitment principle is of no help when there are many options and no compelling reasons for choices. In these cases some form of plausible reasoning is necessary. In general this approach uses more information to control the problem-solving process than the top-down refinement approach [p. 109].
> — Stefik, M., Aikins, J., Balzer, R., Benoit, J., Birnbaum, L., Hayes-Roth, F., and Sacerdoti, E. The organization of expert systems, a tutorial. *Artificial Intelligence, 18*, 135–173 (1982). Copyright 1982, Elsevier Science Publishers B.V.

A second interpretation of constraints is as partial descriptions and *commitments* from the perspective of plan refinement. During the process of planning, there are many opportunities for deciding which part of a plan to make more specific. A least committment approach is to defer decisions as long as possible. A constraint is essentially a partial description of an object; a selection is a full description. By formulating constraints about objects MOLGEN is able to make commitments about partial descriptions of objects without making specific selections.

Constraint formulation is the adding of new constraints as commitments in the design process. A planner can proceed hierarchically by formulating constraints of increasing detail as planning progresses. Thus, a problem solver that can introduce new constraints need not work with all of the details at once. This idea is consistent with the common experience of working on problems that are imprecisely formulated, but which become more tightly specified during the solution process. In contrast, the traditional constraint satisfaction approach works with a fixed number of constraints that are all known at the beginning [pp. 114f.].

MOLGEN differs from constraint satisfaction programs like DENDRAL and REF-ARF in that it is not limited to the initial set of constraints. MOLGEN formulates constraints dynamically as it runs [p. 135].
   — Stefik, M. Planning with constraints (MOLGEN: Part 1). *Artificial Intelligence*, *16*, 111–139 (1981a). Copyright 1981, Elsevier Science Publishers B.V.

A capsule summary of the advantages and disadvantages of Least Commitment as a way of avoiding search by specifying only what can be decided with certainty is as follows:

Least Commitment—MOLGEN [Stefik 1981a,b],

NOAH [Sacerdoti 1977]

- Have to develop a constraint language: *hard*
- Implementation: *hard*
- Computational efficiency: *moderate*
- Forced to search: *Least-Commitment Deadlock (when there are still decisions to be made, but no decision can be made with complete certainty)*

Use the Language of Nonlinear Plans

Rather than requiring plans of action to be linear sequences of actions, we view plans as partial orderings of actions with respect to time. We have demonstrated how, by representing all the freedom of ordering that is innate in a developing plan, a computer system can solve certain problems directly and without backtracking [that is, without search], whereas a linear representation of the plan forces the inefficient use of backtracking [p. 103].

> — Reprinted by permission of the publisher from *A Structure For Plans and Behavior*, by E. D. Sacerdoti. Copyright 1977, Elsevier Science Publishing Co., Inc.

A capsule summary of the advantages and disadvantages of Nonlinear Planning as a way of avoiding search by specifying only what can be decided with certainty is as follows:

Nonlinear Plans—NOAH [Sacerdoti 1977]

- Use partial ordering: *easy*
- Implementation: *moderate difficulty*
- Computational efficiency: *moderate*
- Forced to search: *when the plan is converted to a full ordering so it can be executed*

Top–Down Refinement, Least Commitment, and Heuristic Search

In the following quote Jack Mostow outlines a number of strategies for handling interacting objectives in design tasks. A number of the strategies he mentions are equivalent to the techniques recommended in Guideline 6.7. For example, we consider Mostow's strategy "Defer commitments" to be roughly equivalent to Least Commitment and his "Make critical decisions first" strategy, to be roughly equivalent to Top–Down Refinement. The versions of Heuristic Search referred to in the guideline as *Combining Preference Orderings* and *Break Ties* are paraphrases of Mostow's strategies "Combine orderings" and "Use goals as selection criterion."

Interacting goals can be achieved in several ways, depending on the nature of the interaction. For example, suppose one goal is to implement function F as a VLSI circuit, and another goal is to make the circuit fit on a single chip. Several strategies are possible:

- *Achieve goals sequentially:* First solve one goal, and then transform its solution to achieve the other goal. For example, first implement a circuit to compute F without worrying about area, and then use a compaction algorithm to make it fit on one chip. This strategy runs into difficulty when commitments made in solving the first problem make it hard to solve the second.

- *Defer commitments:* Order the goals so as to start with whichever decisions impose fewest restrictions on the form of the solution. The idea is to postpone decisions not forced by the problem, thereby leaving as much freedom as possible for achieving subsequent goals.

- *Make critical decisions first:* Order the goals so as to start with whichever decisions are most constrained by the problem. For example, design the most constrained component first. Postponing the constrained decision until later in the design would increase the risk of dead ends, since design commitments made in the interim might well render the highly constrained decision over-constrained. By solving the most constrained problem first, before making such commitments, such dead ends can be avoided. This idea is closely related to but distinct from the notion of deferring commitments. The critical path strategy says to make a decision as early as possible if it is highly constrained by the design task, while the deferred commitment strategy says to postpone a decision as long as possible if it is not.

- *Merge goals:* Conjoin the two goals into a single specification and implement it. In the example at hand, that would correspond to the single goal "Implement-F-on-a-chip," which might be useful given methods for solving that goal directly. For this example, however, the strategy appears useless, perhaps because the two goals address such different aspects of the design (functionality and area-efficiency). Goal merging may be more feasible for goals with a common generalization. For example, the goals "implement a circuit to compute $A*x + y$" and "implement a circuit to compute $x + B*y$" can be merged into the single goal "implement a circuit to compute $A*x + B*y$" (assuming one circuit can be shared for both purposes).

- *Use goal as selection criterion:* Use one goal as a criterion for selecting among different solutions to the other, in the hope that the goal being used as the selection criterion will be achieved as well. For example, as the function F is decomposed into primitives that can be implemented in hardware, choose the smallest implementation for each primitive. With luck, the resulting circuit will fit on one chip. This method of integrating two goals is not guaranteed to solve them both.

- *Combine orderings:* If both goals can be used as selection criteria to order some set of choices, they can be combined merging the orderings into a partial or total ordering. For instance, suppose the choices are alternatives for how to implement some function, and the goals are "optimize time" and "optimize space." Each goal induces a different ordering on how the function is implemented. For example, if a goal constrains some resource consumed by the design, it can be used to order implementation alternatives according to some metric on the amount of resources they consume. Two such goals can be merged into a single selection criterion by using some function to combine the two metrics, *e.g.*, "minimize $A*time + B*space$," where A and B reflect the relative importance of the two goals. Alternatively, if one goal is absolutely more important than the other, the secondary goal can be used solely to break ties—*i.e.*, to choose among the alternatives ranked best by the primary goal.

• *Use goal to budget:* Decompose one goal into subgoals parallel with the decomposition of the other. For example, given a decomposition of F into parts, split the total chip area into allocations for each part. If each part is implemented so as to fit into its budgeted area, the circuit will fit. This strategy requires a good decomposition—in this case, an accurate estimate of the area required for each part of the circuit. When such estimates fail, some negotiation is needed to adjust the allocations.

In practice, these control strategies are used in combination. For example, consider the interaction between the goals of testability and area-efficiency in the design of a VLSI chip. A designer might achieve these goals sequentially by first transforming the circuit to make it testable (*i.e.*, make each piece of circuit state settable and observable), and then applying a compaction algorithm to produce an area-efficient layout. However, there are several methods for achieving testability, which vary greatly in the amount of chip area they use. Thus area-efficiency should be used as a selection criterion in choosing among them. Alternatively, the designer might use an area budget, allowing a certain amount of chip area for test circuitry. This constraint would then constrain the solution of the testability goal [Mostow 1985].

   — Reprinted with permission from *AI Magazine*, 1985, pp. 50f., published by the American Association for Artificial Intelligence.

6.8 *Solution: Absolute–Relative–Explanation*

Which of the following best describes the problem you want to pose to your expert system?

(a) **The user will provide a candidate solution and expects the expert system to evaluate the strength of the evidence for and**

against that candidate. (For example: *How much evidence for molybdenum is there?*)

(b) **The user expects the expert system to independently evaluate the evidence for and against each of the candidate solutions, and then either identify the most likely candidates or rank the candidates according to the support each receives.** (For example: *What bacteria are there the most evidence for in this patient?*)

(c) **Rather than considering candidates independently, the user expects the expert system to look for evidence that discriminates between the likely solutions. The expert system should assess the support for the candidates relative to each other.** (For example: *Which of these bacteria is most likely to be causing this illness?*)

(d) **The user expects the expert system to rank candidate solutions according to their ability to provide a coherent and comprehensive explanation of the findings. The emphasis is less on** *selecting* **from a set of alternatives, than it is on** *constructing* **an explanation that shows how one or more candidates combine to produce a satisfactory account of the findings.** (For example: *What bacterial infections would give the best explanation of this illness?*)

Evidence: Any   Type: Any

Evidence for a   → *Yes–No Decision* using *Scoring Functions.*
provided candidate

Type: Preenumerated

Rank according to   → Sequence of independent *Yes–No Decisions.*
absolute amount of
evidence

Type: Preenumerated

A relative standard   → *Group–and–Differentiate*
instead of an absolute
one

Type: Preenumerated, constructed

Explanations   → *Causal Models*

Type: Constructed, simulation

The following two quotes describe the difference between a problem formulated as a sequence of yes–no decisions and a problem formulated as a sequence of tests that discriminate between plausible hypotheses. Both MYCIN and PIP are examples of expert systems that solve problems involving a sequence of binary decisions, and this approach is contrasted with the Group-and-Differentiate approach taken by INTERNIST.

> Ordinary Bayesian task formulations, structured as differential diagnoses, require the assumption that one and only one of the diseases in the differential list is present in the case. This conventional problem structure entails one task and one decision, whereas a formulation based on a binary choice (between X and not X) [that is, a yes–no decision] entails n tasks (where n is the total number of diseases known to the system) and permits as many as n positive conclusions.

> Problem solving procedures for making true/false judgments concerning evoked hypotheses may be of many forms. As already noted, a method commonly employed is that of statistical decision theory. An interesting variant is that of MYCIN, which employs an adaptation of the theorem proving methods of AI to "prove" (up to a specified certainty level) the truth or falsity of each considered hypothesis.

> There is nothing particularly demanding about the control strategy required for managing the consideration of a succession of binary choice tasks. The program can be set up in a straightforward fashion to proceed sequentially through the list of possibilities, considering each in turn, accumulating evidence for and against the hypothesis in accordance with the specified problem solving procedure.

> The main difficulty with the binary choice approach is that it fails to aggregate possibilities into decision sets; instead, each considered diagnosis is evaluated as though independent of all other alternatives. This requires absolute criteria for decision making, as the problem solver is denied access to the powerful heuristics ... that enable decisions to be rendered relative to a postulated decision set.

> These heuristics, which provide guidance to the physician concerning the need for additional discriminating information and permit the use of efficient decision strategies such as "the process of elimination" [called "Confirmation by Exclusion" in this book] can be used only in the context of tasks structured as differential diagnoses [Pople 1982, pp. 130f.].

— Pople, H. E., Jr. Heuristic methods for imposing structure on ill-structured problems: The structuring of medical diagnostics. In *Artificial Intelligence in Medicine*, P. Szolovits (ed). Boulder, CO: Westview Press, American Association for the Advancement of Science, 1982, pp. 119–190. Copyright 1982, American Association for the Advancement of Science. Reprinted by permission.

To compare the strengths and weaknesses of two different approaches to medical diagnosis, Howard Sherman wrote two expert systems that both used the same knowledge base of birth-defect symptoms. One of his expert systems was modeled after the PIP program [Pauker, Gorry, Kassirer, and Schwartz 1976] and the other, after the INTERNIST program [Pople, Myers, and Miller 1975]. While the PIP algorithm was superior in some respects, the following quote argues that the relative criterion employed by INTERNIST has advantages for detecting the correct birth defect. Sherman also studied the value of a questioning strategy that attempts to widen the difference between the top two hypotheses by asking for information that would increase support for one hypothesis at the expense of the other hypotheses. Given that a relative standard is adopted for hypothesis selection, he shows that this differentiation strategy produces a statistically significant improvement in system performance [pp. 72–75]. Taken together, these results suggest that the Group–and–Differentiate strategy has advantages for finding the best hypothesis over a simple strategy of ranking the amount of evidence in favor of each hypothesis considered independently.

References to INTERNIST and PIP in the following quote refer to Sherman's INTERNIST-like program and his PIP-like program as opposed to the originals.

PIP and INTERNIST take a simple solution to the problem of when to conclude that a syndrome is present. They use the scores of the hypotheses and a predetermined threshold value. As stated before, PIP requires that a hypothesis' score exceeds the threshold while INTERNIST requires that the difference between the scores of the top two hypotheses exceeds the threshold. To evaluate these two methods, the hypotheses concluded by each system were examined.

The results showed that INTERNIST concluded the correct syndrome in 34 of the 35 cases and in one case no syndrome was concluded. PIP, on the other hand, concluded the correct syndrome in thirty cases, failed to conclude any syndrome in four cases, and concluded an incorrect syndrome in two cases.[2]

[2]In one case PIP concluded both a correct and an incorrect syndrome.

The differences in the number of incorrect syndromes concluded and the number of cases where no syndromes were concluded, although not statistically significant, can be explained by differences in the algorithms. In both of the cases where PIP concluded an incorrect syndrome there was another hypothesis which had a score that was very close. INTERNIST would not have concluded the syndrome at that point since it uses the difference between the scores of the leading hypotheses and not the actual magnitude of the leading hypothesis' score.

In the three cases where PIP failed to conclude any syndrome but INTERNIST did conclude the correct syndrome, PIP was pursuing the correct hypothesis but due to stray and/or absent findings (quite common in birth defects) the correct hypothesis score was not greater than the threshold for confirmation. In INTERNIST, although the magnitude of the correct hypothesis was not very large, the difference between its score and those of the other hypotheses was great enough to conclude the correct hypotheses.

In summary, it appears that considering the score of the leading hypothesis alone is not as effective in determining when to confirm that the hypothesis is present as considering its score relative to the score of the other hypotheses [Sherman 1981, pp. 63f.].
  — Copyright 1981, Massachusetts Institute of Technology. Reprinted by permission.

The following two quotes discuss the problem of constructing coherent explanations of medical symptoms that was tackled by the ABEL expert system and contrasts this problem with the Group–and–Differentiate problem addressed by INTERNIST.

From our experience with the existing diagnostic systems [Pauker, Gorry, Kassirer, and Schwartz 1976; Pople, Myers, and Miller 1975], we are convinced that a relatively simple representation of physician's analysis of patient's illness (i.e., a list of disease hypotheses) is incapable of providing the desired level of expertise. The patient description must unify all known facts about the patient, their interpretations, their suspected interrelationships, and disease hypotheses in order to explain these findings [p. 896].
  — Patil, R. S., Szolovits, P., and Schwartz, W. B. Causal understanding of patient illness in medical diagnosis. *Proceedings of the Seventh International Joint Conference on Artificial Intelligence*, 1981, pp. 893–899. Used by permission of the International Joint Conferences on Artificial Intelligence, Inc.; copies of this and other IJCAI Proceedings are available from Morgan Kaufmann Publishers, Inc., PO Box 50490, Palo Alto, CA 94303, USA.

These observations have led to a re-evaluation of the techniques used in the first generation of AIM [Artificial Intelligence in Medicine] programs. The following insights have been gained by this evaluation. Firstly, the notion of causality is inadequately exploited in the first generation AIM programs [Smith 1978, Patil 1979, Pople 1982]. They do not utilize the structure provided by causal relations to organize the patient facts and disease hypotheses. They fail to capture the human notion that explanation should rest on a chain of cause–effect deduction. Secondly, they cannot deal with the effects of more than one disease present in a patient simultaneously, especially when one of the diseases alters the presentation of the others. Thirdly, they do not deal with the knowledge of a disease phenomenon at different levels of detail that a physician clearly has. Finally, the numeric belief measures as used by the first generation AIM programs do not provide adequate criteria for diagnostic reasoning. They are unable to capture notions such as adequacy and parsimony of a diagnostic possibility [p. 9].

It is one of the central themes of this thesis that these problems cannot be avoided by relying solely on the numerical scoring mechanism; the programs must be provided with structural criteria to evaluate the disease hypotheses [p. 11] [Patil 1981].

7 Knowledge Representation

The guidelines in this chapter indicate that in some cases the type of knowledge available determines the type of reasoning methods employed, while in other cases the type of reasoning methods required determines the knowledge representation employed. Guideline 7.1 is an example of a case where characteristics of the available knowledge determine the reasoning methods.

7.1 Degree of Structure in Knowledge

What is the appropriate characterization of the knowledge available in this domain?

1. **There is a poorly structured collection of many isolated facts. It is unclear what kinds of distinctions between facts are the important ones.**

2. **There is a complex, highly structured collection of facts and relationships. There is a rich and fairly well established set of distinctions made between different kinds of information.**

3. There is a concise, unified theory.

Evidence: Any   Type: Any

Poorly structured collection of isolated facts	→ Use *Rules* or *Assertions* to represent the knowledge.
Structured set of knowledge	→ Use *Frames* or *Semantic Networks* to represent the knowledge.
Concise, unified theory	→ Use *Mathematics* or *Algorithms* to represent the knowledge.

Guideline 7.2 also exemplifies the impact of knowledge on reasoning in that it recommends different reasoning methods depending on whether the available knowledge consists of heuristics, constraints, examples, or models. The need to represent knowledge economically can also place demands on the reasoning processes as exemplified by Guidelines 7.3, 7.4, and 7.5. These guidelines consider the advisability of complicating retrieval routines in various ways to save on storage—another case of the familiar space–time trade-off.

Other guidelines exemplify the reverse impact of reasoning methods on knowledge representation. For example, Guideline 7.6 enquires about the possibility that problem-solving will consist of finding paths of particular kinds through the expert system's knowledge base. To support this path-finding process, the knowledge is frequently cast in the form of explicit networks. Guideline 7.7 considers a variety of problem-solving methods and indicates the knowledge representation scheme that best supports each of those reasoning methods.

7.1.1 Support for Example Guideline 7.1

The following quote describes the decision not to represent the MYCIN knowledge base in a Semantic Net formalism because the knowledge consisted of a poorly structured collection of isolated facts.

> There is little doubt that the decision to use rules to encode infectious disease knowledge in the nascent MYCIN system was largely influenced by experience in using similar techniques in DENDRAL. However, ...

we did experiment with a semantic network representation before turning to the production rule model. The impressive published examples of Carbonell's SCHOLAR system [Carbonell 1970a,b], with its ability to carry on a mixed-initiative dialogue regarding the geography of South America, seemed to us a useful model of the kind of rich interactive environment that would be needed for a system to advise physicians.

Our disenchantment with a pure semantic network representation of domain knowledge arose for several reasons as we began to work with Cohen and Axline, our collaborating experts. First, the knowledge of infectious disease therapy selection was ill-structured and, we found, difficult to represent using labeled arcs between nodes. Unlike South American geography, our domain did not have a clear-cut hierarchical organization, and we found it challenging to transfer a page or two from a medical textbook into a network of sufficient richness for our purposes.

Perhaps the greatest problem with a network representation, and the greatest appeal of production rules, was our gradually recognized need to deal with small chunks of domain knowledge in interacting with our expert collaborators. Because they were not used to dissecting their clinical reasoning processes, it was totally useless to ask them to "tell us everything you know." However, by discussing specific difficult patients, and by encouraging our collaborators to justify their questions or decisions, those of us who were not expert in the field began to tease out "nuggets" of domain knowledge—individual inferential facts that the experts identified as pertinent for problem solving in the domain. By encoding these facts as individual production rules, rather than attempting to decompose them into nodes and links in a semantic network, we found that the experts were able to examine and critique the rules without difficulty [Buchanan and Shortliffe 1984, pp. 55f.].

> — Buchanan/Shortliffe, *Rule-Based Expert Systems*, © 1984 by B. G. Buchanan and E. H. Shortliffe. Reprinted with permission of Addison-Wesley Publishing Co., Inc., Reading, Massachusetts.

The following quote discusses the inability of rule-based systems to distinguish between different kinds of facts.

Our experience using EMYCIN to build several expert systems has suggested some negative aspects to using such a simple representation for all the knowledge. The associations that are encoded in rules are elemental and cannot be further examined (except through the symbolic text stored in slots such as JUSTIFICATION or AUTHOR). A reasoning program using only homogeneous rules with no internal distinctions among them thus fails to distinguish among:

Chance associations (e.g., proportionally more left-handed than right-handed persons have been infected by *E. coli* at our institution)

Statistical correlations (e.g., meningococcal meningitis outbreaks are correlated with crowded living conditions)

Heuristics based on experience rather than precise statistical studies (e.g., oral administration of drugs is less reliable in children than are injections)

Causal associations (e.g., streptomycin can cause deafness)

Definitions (e.g., all *E. coli* are gram-negative rods)

Knowledge about structure (e.g., the mouth is connected to the pharynx)

Taxonomic knowledge (e.g., viral meningitis is a kind of infection)

The success of MYCIN, which generally does not distinguish among these types of associations, demonstrates that it is possible to build a high-performance program within a sparse representation of homogeneous rules (augmented with a few other knowledge structures). Nevertheless, limited experience with CENTAUR, WHEEZE, NEOMYCIN, and ONCOCIN leads us to believe that the tasks of building, maintaining, and understanding the knowledge base will be easier if the types of knowledge are separated. This becomes especially pertinent during knowledge acquisition ... and when teaching the knowledge base to students.

Many problems require richer distinctions or finer control than MYCIN-like rules provide. A more general representation, such as frames, allows a system designer to make the description of the world more complex. In frames, for instance, it is easier to express the following:

- Procedural knowledge—sequencing tasks

- Control knowledge—when to invoke knowledge sources

- Knowledge of context—the general context in which elements of the knowledge base are relevant

- Inheritance of properties—automatic transfer of values of some slots from parent concepts to offspring

- Distinctions among types of links—parent and offspring concepts may be linked as

  o class and instance

  o whole and part

  o set and subset

The loss of simplicity in the frame representation, however, may complicate the inference, explanation, and knowledge acquisition routines. For example, inheritance of properties will be handled (and explained) differently depending on the type of link between parent and offspring concepts.

There is a trade-off between simplicity and expressive power. A simpler representation is easier to use but constrains the kinds of things a system builder might want to say. There is also a trade-off between generality and the power of knowledge acquisition tools. An unconstrained representation may have the expressive power of a programming language such as LISP or assembly language, but it can be more difficult to debug. There is considerable overlap among the alternative representation methods, and current work in AI is still experimenting with different ways of making this trade-off [Buchanan and Shortliffe 1984, pp. 675–677].

— Buchanan/Shortliffe, *Rule-Based Expert Systems*, © 1984 by B. G. Buchanan and E. H. Shortliffe. Reprinted with permission of Addison-Wesley Publishing Co., Inc., Reading, Massachusetts.

We can imagine two very different classes of problems—the first is best viewed and understood as consisting of many independent states, while the second seems best understood via a concise, unified theory, perhaps embodied in a single law. Examples of the former include some views of perceptual psychology or clinical medicine, in which there are many states relative to the number of actions (this may be due either to our lack of a cohesive theory or to the basic complexity of the system being modeled). Examples of the latter include well-established areas of physics and mathematics, in which a few basic tenets serve to embody much of the required knowledge, and in which the discovery of unifying principles has emphasized the similarities in seemingly different states. This first distinction appears to be one important factor in distinguishing appropriate from inappropriate domains.

A second distinction concerns the complexity of control flow. At two extremes, we can imagine two processes, one of which is a set of independent actions and the other of which is a complex collection of multiple, parallel processes involving several dependent subprocesses.

A third distinction concerns the extent to which the knowledge to be embedded in a system can be separated from the manner in which it is to be used [also known as the controversy between declarative and procedural representations; see Winograd [1975] for an extensive discussion]. As one example, we can imagine simply stating facts, perhaps in a language like predicate calculus, without assuming how those facts will be employed. Alternatively, we could write procedural descriptions of how to accomplish a stated goal. Here the use of the knowledge is for the most part predetermined during the process of embodying it in this representation.

In all three of these distinctions, a PS [Production System, that is, a Rule interpreter] is well-suited to the first description and ill-suited to the latter. The existence of multiple, nontrivially different, independent states is an indication of the feasibility of writing multiple, nontrivial, modular rules. A process composed of a set of independent actions requires only limited communication between the actions, and as we shall see, this is an important characteristic of PS's. The ability to state what knowledge ought to be in the system without also describing its use greatly improves the ease with which a PS can be written ... [Davis and King 1975, p. 10].
— Reprinted by permission of author.

7.2 Type of Knowledge

What kinds of knowledge are available:

1. Heuristic rules of thumb?

2. Constraints that describe or specify an acceptable solution?

3. Examples of problems and their solutions?

4. Models that describe structure and function?

Evidence: Any   Type: Any

Heuristics → *Rules* whose left-hand sides describe findings or abstractions of findings and whose right-hand sides propose solutions or solution features; that is, *Heuristic Associations*.

Evidence: Weak, moderate

Constraints → *Constraint Propagation* or use a *Theorem Prover* to prove that a candidate solution satisfies the constraints.

Examples → *Case-Based Reasoning*, usually involving some form of *Partial Matching* {expensive}.

> Evidence: Weak, moderate   Type: Preenumerated, constructed

Models → *Causal Models*

> Type: Constructed, simulation

These alternatives are not mutually exclusive, as problems are likely to have various mixes of these different kinds of knowledge.

Rules

Rule-based programs can be easier to modify than conventional programs. This is particularly likely to be the case if the rule set is small (say, less than 100 rules) and there is limited interaction between the rules. Ease of modification is important when encoding the heuristic knowledge of experts. Experts are only imperfectly aware of their own heuristics, and many changes to the statement of a heuristic may be required before it accurately reflects the experts' own behavior. The following two quotes recommend rules for encoding domain-dependent, heuristic knowledge. The first quote is from a paper describing CRYSALIS, an expert system that infers the three-dimensional structures of molecules from X-ray diffraction data.

> The method of interpreting protein EDM's [electron-density maps] is, at its critical points, opportunistic. Where to start, when to leave one part of the structure and focus upon another, what level of detail to look at, when to stop—these questions are continually presented to the expert as he builds his structure. The knowledge needed to answer them is almost entirely heuristic, and as subject to change as any other task-specific knowledge. It thus seems natural, and indeed has shown to be practical, that this strategic knowledge, which controls the order in which various tasks are performed, be represented as rules [Engelmore and Terry 1979, p. 255].

> The important link we have added is a heuristic association between a characterization of the patient ("compromised host") and categories of diseases ("gram-negative infection"). Unlike definitional and hierarchical inferences, this inference makes a great leap. A *heuristic relation* is uncertain, based on assumptions of typicality, and is sometimes just a poorly understood correlation. A heuristic is often empirical, deriving

from problem-solving experience; heuristics correspond to the "rules of thumb," often associated with expert systems [Feigenbaum 1977].

To summarize, in heuristic classification abstracted data statements are associated with specific problem solutions or features that characterize a solution [Clancey 1985, pp. 294f.].

Case-Based Reasoning

The problem with examples as a source of knowledge is that they are unlikely to occur again at any time, identical in all their particulars, nor is it generally clear what features of an example were crucial to its successful solution. For these reasons a Partial Matcher may be employed to find the examples that are most similar to the current case of interest. This involves relying on the generally applicable heuristic that the more similar two examples are, the more likely it is that their solutions are also similar. The following quote describes the TAXMAN system, which has been applied to problems in legal reasoning. The TAXMAN system's source of knowledge consists of examples of legal cases and Partial Matching has been employed to determine the relevance of these examples.

Lawyers would object, however, that the logical template model is theoretically inadequate as a representation of a system of legal concepts. First, a lawyer might say, the most important legal concepts are "open-textured" (see Hart [1961, pp. 121–150]): their structure is never logical and precise, but amorphous and poorly defined. Second, legal concepts are not static structures, but dynamic ones (see Dworkin [1975]): they are typically constructed and reconstructed as they are applied to a particular set of facts. In this paper we will describe a representation of a system of legal concepts which attempts to capture some of these characteristics. In place of the logical template model, we will represent an abstract concept by a *prototype* and a sequence of *deformations* of the prototype: the prototype is a relatively concrete description selected from the lower-level factual network itself, and the deformations are selected from among the possible *mappings* of one concrete description into another [p. 246].

As a step toward the implementation of the prototype-plus-deformation representation, we have extended the pattern-matching procedures to deal with partial matches, and we have added several heuristics to produce a plausible version of a "best match" result [p. 252].

— McCarty, L. T., and Sridharan, N. S. The representation of an evolving system of legal concepts: II. Prototypes and deformations. *Proceedings of the Seventh International Joint Conference on Artificial Intelligence*, 1981, pp. 246–253. Used by permission of the International Joint Conferences on

Artificial Intelligence, Inc.; copies of this and other IJCAI Proceedings are available from Morgan Kaufmann Publishers, Inc., PO Box 50490, Palo Alto, CA 94303, USA.

7.3 Instances Inherit Default Properties

On the average, do we know five or more new facts about a domain object simply by being told that it is of Type X?

or

Are these new facts not known with certainty, but assumed unless there is evidence to the contrary?

Evidence: Any   Type: Any

Yes → Place the object in a data structure (e.g., *Frames*, *Semantic Nets*, or *Objects*) whose *Inheritance Mechanisms* will provide the facts when needed, and whose *Default Values* will be assumed unless an exception is explicitly asserted.

Neither → Assert the new facts explicitly {cheap}.

Schemes for implicitly representing facts generally have the ability to represent defaults, that is, facts not known with certainty, but assumed unless there is information to the contrary. One way to represent a default is to represent it implicitly. If it turns out that there is information to the contrary, then that contrary information is explicitly asserted, and this has the consequence of overruling the default.

Knowledge bases are distinguished from databases primarily by virtue of the possibility that relationships may be based on *implicit* computations. Consider, for example, a "citizenship" relationship between individuals and companies. An American corporation may wish to indicate that the citizenship of an employee is the United States unless explicitly stated otherwise. This may be achieved by declaring an entity which represents the *class* of all employees and defining the "citizenship" relationship on that class to be "U.S.A." Entities corresponding to individual employees are then declared to be *instances* of that class object. If no explicit "citizenship" relationship is given for an instance, that relationship is *inherited* from the class object; however, it is possible to override the inheritance for any specific instance by explicitly defining the "citizenship" relationship on that instance.

This implicit computation of relationships is of great value in the domain of [oil well] log interpretation. The complexity of the task is such that it is seldom the case that the most fundamental relationships regarding information about tool behavior or geology can be given explicitly. Such information can only be derived on the basis of knowledge of what information is available; and, even then, the results of such derivations may necessitate revision. Thus, knowledge bases provide an appropriate framework for the representation of the "states of knowledge" through which a log analyst must pass in the course of problem solving [Baker and Smoliar 1984, p. 559].
— © 1984 by IEEE. Reprinted by permission.

When designing a DS [data structure], it is possible to provide mechanisms for holding a vast amount of information *implicitly*. In AM, e.g., the organization of concepts into a Genl/Spec hierarchy (plus the assumed heritability properties; ...) permits a rule to ask for "all concepts more general than primes" as if that were a piece of data explicitly stored in a DS. In fact, only direct generalizations are stored ("the immediate generalization of primes is numbers"), and a "rippling" mechanism automatically runs up the Genl links to assemble a complete answer. Thus the number of specific answers the DS can provide is far greater than the number of individual items in the DS. True, these DS mechanisms will use up extra time in processing to obtain the answer; this is efficient since any particular request is very unlikely to be made [Lenat and Harris 1978, pp. 45f.].
— Copyright 1978, Academic Press. Reprinted by permission.

7.4 Overlap in Factual Knowledge

In any one problem will it be necessary to reason about a number of different instances of the same kind of object? (For example: *The expert system might have to reason about several different aircraft all of the same kind.*)

   and

Will it be necessary to be aware of important differences between instances despite their commonalities? (For example: *Instances of the same kind of aircraft might differ in fuel aboard, assignments, or readiness.*)

Evidence: Any   Type: Any

Yes → Use *Frames*, the *Objects* of *Object-Oriented Programming*, or *EMYCIN Contexts* to represent the instances.

The general problem is to capture commonalities without obscuring important differences. In a medical expert system each individual patient can be an instance of the Patient frame (or the Patient object or the Patient context), and this captures the common features of all patients in an economical way. At the same time the slots of a particular instance frame (or the instance variables of an Patient object or the parameters of a Patient context) can be used to record information that distinguishes patients from each other.

If there are no important differences between instances, then the use of frames or objects or contexts is unwarranted. In this case, naming conventions generally suffice to indicate the required discriminations. For example, the assertion "The infection is *E. coli*" distinguishes *E. coli* from other bacteria but makes no distinctions between cases of *E. coli*. This is appropriate if all *E. coli* is pretty much alike as far as the system is concerned. In this case, representing each case of *E. coli* as an instance of the *E. coli* frame involves unnecessary expense.

> The primary reason for defining additional context-types in a consultant [i.e., an expert system] is to represent multiple instances of an entity during a case. Some users may like to define context-types that always have one instance and no more, primarily for purposes of organization, but this is often unnecessary (and even cumbersome).[1] For example, one might want to write rules that use various attributes of a patient's liver, but since there is always exactly one liver for a patient there is no need to have a liver context; any attribute of the liver can simply be viewed as an attribute of the patient [Buchanan and Shortliffe 1984, p. 500].
> — Buchanan/Shortliffe, *Rule-Based Expert Systems*, © 1984 by B. G. Buchanan and E. H. Shortliffe. Reprinted with permission of Addison-Wesley Publishing Co., Inc., Reading, Massachusetts.

7.5 Overlapping Capabilities

Will the expert system need to represent the capabilities and behaviors of a number of objects?

---

[1]Note, however, that separating unique concepts out into single contexts may provide more understandable rule translations due to the conventions of context-name substitutions in text generation. See Scott, Clancey, Davis, and Shortliffe [1977] for further discussion of this point.

and

Are there significant commonalities among the capabilities and behaviors of different objects?

Evidence: Any   Type: Constructed, simulation

Yes → Define new *Objects* (in the *Object-Oriented Programming* sense) whose capabilities are the shared capabilities of the original objects. Have the original objects *Inherit* their common capabilities from the newly defined objects. Differences between objects inheriting common capabilities are represented by overruling the inherited information or elaborating on the inherited information.

The power of flavors (and the name "flavors") comes from the ability to mix several flavors and get a new flavor. Since the functionality of **ship** and **meteor** partially overlap, we can take the common functionality and move it into its own flavor, which might be called **moving-object**.

What we have done here is to take an abstract type, **moving-object**, and build two more specialized and powerful abstract types on top of it. Any ship or meteor can do anything a moving object can do, and each also has its own specific abilities [Stallman, Weinreb, and Moon 1983, pp. 411–412].
— Reprinted by permission of author.

The behaviors of basic objects often have many commonalities that are revealed in the process of defining their behaviors. For example, GCI's [ground control intercept radars], AWACS [airborne radars], and SAMs [surface-to-air missiles] all share the ability to detect, and their detection behaviors are identical. We can take advantage of ROSS's inheritance hierarchy (see McArthur and Klahr [1982]) to reorganize object behaviors in a way that both emphasizes these conceptual similarities and eliminates redundant code. For example, for objects that have the behaviors of detection in common, we define a more abstract generic object called RADAR to store these common behaviors. We then place it above GCI, AWACS, and SAM in the hierarchy, so that they automatically inherit the behavior for detection whenever necessary. Hence we avoid writing these behaviors separately three times.

Each object type in the class hierarchy can be construed as a description or view of the objects below it. One object (AWACS) happens to inherit its behaviors along more than one branch of the hierarchy (via

RADAR and MOVING-OBJECT). Such "multiple views" or "multiple inheritance" is possible in ROSS but not in most other object-oriented programming environments [multiple inheritance is more common now than when this was written] [Klahr, McArthur, and Narain 1982, p. 333].
— Reprinted with permission from *Proceedings of the National Conference on Artificial Intelligence*, 1982, pp. 331–334, published by the American Association for Artificial Intelligence.

7.6 Networks of Knowledge

Do the facts needed to solve problems in this domain consist of a large, set of statements involving a few kinds of semantic relationships? (For example: *causes/caused-by, is-a-kind-of, if–then*)

and

Does the reasoning required to solve this problem depend on the *patterns* **defined by these relationships?** (For example: *a chain of* is-a *links, a connected path of causal links, etc.*)

Evidence: Any   Type: Any

Yes → Represent the facts with *Semantic Networks*. (Also called *Causal Networks* or *Inference Networks*, depending on the type of relationship involved.)

The following quotes illustrate that the structural patterns defined by semantic relationships can often be conveniently processed by various kinds of graph search, for example, spreading activation or causal chain construction.

> The significance of this graphical representation is that it allows certain kinds of inference to be performed by simple graph-searching techniques. For example, to find out if a particular individual has a certain attribute, it is sufficient to search from the constant representing that individual, up *is-a* links, for a node having an edge labelled with the attribute. By placing the attribute as high as possible in the taxonomy, all individuals below it can *inherit* the property.

> In addition, the graph representation suggests different kinds of inference that are based more directly on the structure of the KB [Knowledge Base] than on its logical content. For example, we can ask how

two nodes are related and answer by finding a path in the graph between them. Given for instance, Clyde the elephant and Jimmy Carter, we could end up with an answer saying that Clyde is an elephant and that the favorite food of elephants is peanuts which is also the product of the farm owned by Jimmy Carter. A typical method of producing this answer would be to perform a "spreading activation" search beginning at the nodes for Clyde and Jimmy. Obviously this form of question would be very difficult to answer for a KB that was not in semantic net form [Levesque 1984, p. 149].

> — Levesque, H. J. A fundamental tradeoff in knowledge representation and reasoning. *Proceedings of the Fourth Conference of the Canadian Society for Computational Studies of Intelligence*, London, Ontario, 1984, pp. 141–152. Copyright 1984, Canadian Society for Computational Studies of Intelligence. Reprinted by permission.

The CASNET or causal–associational network is a particular type of semantic network designed to:

- describe a disease in causal terms

- relate this description to an associational structure of observations (e.g., symptoms and test results)

- describe various classifications imposed on the model (e.g., diagnoses and treatments)

Events are related in the form *A causes B*, and reasoning methods in CASNET take advantage of the causal ordering, although in a somewhat different manner than would be carried out with pure production rules. With causal ordering information, one can deduce the most likely cause that accounts for a particular set of patient data by using an algorithm that traverses the "network" of plausible causes and effects, and finds those causes that, if present, would produce the largest number of observed effects.

Once the inference of intraocular pressure elevation is made, its causal relationships to other intermediate states are pursued, and when a sufficiently strong causal path has been connected, the diagnostic conclusions are inferred through classification tables or sets of rules that interpret patterns over the causal network [Weiss and Kulikowski 1984, pp. 44f.].

> — Copyright 1984, Sholom M. Weiss and Casimir A. Kulikowski. Reprinted by permission.

A collection of rules about some specific subject area invariably uses the same pieces of evidence to imply several different hypotheses. It also frequently happens that alternative pieces of evidence imply the same hy-

pothesis. Furthermore, there are often chains of evidences and hypotheses. For these reasons it is natural to represent a collection of rules as a graph structure or *inference net* [Duda, Hart, and Nilsson 1976, p. 1076].
  — Copyright 1976, American Federation of Information Processing Societies, Inc. Reprinted by permission.

7.7 *Organize Knowledge to Support Reasoning*

All the previous guidelines were of the form

If ⟨Problem Characteristic⟩, then use ⟨Implementation Technique⟩

In this section, for the first time, we see a design guideline of the form

If ⟨Implementation Technique 1⟩,

then use ⟨Implementation Technique 2⟩

Chapter 8 will also present guidelines of this form, whenever Implementation Technique 2 remedies a problem inherent in the use of Implementation Technique 1.

What reasoning strategy has been selected for use in this expert system?

1. **Goal-Driven Reasoning or Data-Driven Reasoning**

2. **Group–and–Differentiate**

3. **Meta-Level Reasoning to select a reasoning strategy**

4. **Opportunistic Search**

5. **Top–Down Refinement or Least Commitment**

Evidence: Any   Type: Any

Goal-Driven Reasoning or Data-Driven Reasoning	→ Structure the Knowledge Base into *Hierarchies of Hypotheses* from general to specific.
Group–and–Differentiate	→ Structure the Knowledge Base into *Multiple Hierarchies of Hypotheses* based on different dimensions.
Meta-Level Reasoning to select a reasoning strategy	→ Structure the Knowledge Base to distinguish different types of relationships between evidence and hypotheses or index strategies by the type of tasks they are best suited for.
Opportunistic Search	→ Organize hypotheses into *Levels of Abstraction*. Index operators by both the hypothesis levels they get their inputs from and the hypothesis levels they write their outputs to.
Top–Down Refinement or Least Commitment	→ Structure the Knowledge Base into a *Hierarchy of Operators* from general to specific.

Several of the items in the following quote from William Clancey have been combined in the recommendations of Guideline 7.7. For example, the first two items in the quote have been combined since they lead to the same recommendation, *Hierarchies of Hypotheses*. Also, the fourth (NEOMYCIN) and seventh (AM) items have been combined since, in our estimation, they are both concerned with Meta-Level Reasoning to select a reasoning strategy.

> One product of this study is a characterization of different ways of structuring KS's [Knowledge Sources] for different strategical purposes. In all cases, the effect of the structural knowledge is to provide a handle for separating out what the KS is from when it is to be applied.[2] The different ways of structuring KS's are summarized here according to the processing rationale:

[2]In this section, the term *hypothesis* generally refers to a diagnostic or explanatory interpretation made by a KS (in terms of some model), although it can also be a hypothesis that a particular problem feature is present.

(a) *Organize KS's hierarchically by hypothesis for consistency in data-directed interpretation.* In DENDRAL, if a functional group is ruled out, more specific members of the family are not considered during forward-directed, preliminary interpretation of spectral peaks. Without this organization of KS's, earlier versions of DENDRAL could generate a subgroup as a plausible interpretation while ruling out a more general form of the subgroup, as if to say "This is an ethyl ketone but not a ketone" [Buchanan, Sutherland, and Feigenbaum 1970].

(b) *Organize KS's hierarchically by hypothesis to eliminate redundant effort in hypothesis-directed refinement.* In DENDRAL, the family trees prevent the exhaustive structure generator from generating subgroups whose more general forms have been ruled out. The same principle is basic to most medical diagnosis systems that organize diagnoses in a taxonomy and use a top–down refinement strategy, such as CENTAUR and NEOMYCIN.

(c) *Organize KS's by multiple hypothesis hierarchies for efficient grouping (hypothesis–space splitting).* Besides using the hierarchy of generic disease processes (infectious, cancerous, toxic, traumatic, psychosomatic, etc.), NEOMYCIN groups the same diseases by multiple hierarchies according to disease process features (organ system involved, spread in the system, progression over time, etc.). When hypotheses are under consideration that do not fall into one confirmed subtree of the primary etiological hierarchy, the 'group and differentiate' strategy is invoked to find a process feature dimension along which two or more current hypotheses differ. A question will then be asked, or a hypothesis pursued, to differentiate among the hypotheses on this dimension.

(d) *Organize KS's for each hypothesis on the basis of how KS data relates to the hypothesis, for focusing on problem features.* In NEOMYCIN, additional relations make explicit special kinds of connections between data and hypotheses, such as "this problem feature is the enabling causal step for this diagnostic process" and meta-rules order the selection of questions (invocation of KS's) by indexing them indirectly through these relations. For example, "If an enabling causal step is known for the hypothesis to be confirmed, try to confirm that problem feature." The meta-rules that reference these different relations ("enabling step," "trigger," "most likely manifestation") are ordered arbitrarily. Meta–meta-rules don't order the meta-rules because we currently have no theoretical basis for relating the first-order relations to one another.

(e) *Organize KS's into data/hypothesis levels for opportunistic triggering at multiple levels of interpretation.* HEARSAY's blackboard levels (sentence, word sequence, word, etc.) organize KS's by the level of analysis they use for data, each level supplying data for the hypothesis level above it. When new results are posted on a given level, KS's that "care about" that level of analysis are polled to see if they should be given processing time. *Policy KS's* give coherence to this opportunistic invocation by affecting which levels will be given preference. CRYSALIS [Engelmore and Terry, 1979] (a program that constructs a three-dimensional crystal structure interpretation of x-ray crystallographic data) takes the idea a step further by having multiple planes of blackboards; one abstracts problem features, and the other abstracts interpretations.

(f) *Organize KS's into a task hierarchy for planning.* In MOLGEN, laboratory operators are referenced indirectly through tasks that are steps in an abstract plan. For example, the planning level *design decision* to refine the abstract plan step MERGE is accomplished by indexing laboratory operators by the MERGE task (e.g., MERGE could be refined to using a ligase to connect DNA structures, mixing solutions, or causing a vector to be absorbed by an organism). Thus tasks in planning are analogous to hypotheses in interpretation problems.

(g) *Organize KS's into a context specialization hierarchy for determining task relevance.* In AM, relevant heuristics for a task are inherited from all concepts that appear above it in the specialization hierarchy. Thus AM goes a step beyond most other systems by showing that policy KS's must be selected on the basis of the kind of problem being solved. Lenat's work suggests that this might be simply a hierarchical relationship among kinds of problems.

[pp. 242–245].
— Clancey, W. J. Extensions to rules for explanation and tutoring. *Artificial Intelligence, 20,* 215–251 (1983). Copyright 1983, Elsevier Science Publishers B.V.

8 Pitfalls of the Implementation Techniques

The design guidelines presented in this book recommend a variety of AI techniques. This chapter describes some of the potential pitfalls associated with these techniques. When techniques exist that overcome the pitfalls, they are also described. Not every technique recommended in Chapters 2 through 7 is listed in this chapter. Although it seems likely that every technique has some sort of pitfall, only those pitfalls that are well established are described here.

Sometimes a technique is listed as the remedy for a pitfall, and that remedy itself has a pitfall associated with it. For example, Subjective Bayesian Methods are a remedy for a problem with Bayes Rule, but Subjective Bayesian Methods also have problems associated with them. In this case, the alphabetical ordering is violated, and the problem with Subjective Bayesian Methods is listed immediately following its listing as a remedy for the Bayes Rule problem.

8.1 Bayes Rule

Bayes Rule

has the problem

that it involves an assumption of conditional independence among findings.

The assumption of conditional independence of symptoms usually does not apply and can lead to substantial errors in certain settings [Norusis and Jacquez 1975]. This has led some investigators to seek new numerical techniques that avoid the independence assumption [Cumberpatch and Heaps 1976]. If a pure Bayesian formulation is used without making the independence assumption, however, the number of required conditional probabilities become prohibitive for complex real-world problems. [Szolovits and Pauker 1978] [Shortliffe, Buchanan, and Feigenbaum 1979, p. 1216].

Bayes Rule

has the problem that a

large amount of data is required to determine all the conditional probabilities needed in the rigorous application of the formula [Kunz, Shortliffe, Buchanan, & Feigenbaum 1983, p. 9].
— Reprinted by permission of author.

Remedy: **Subjective Bayesian Methods.**

Typically, an ad hoc scoring function is used to combine the effects of collections of uncertain evidence acting through several inference rules on the same hypothesis. Thus, rule-based systems attempt to substitute judgments distilled from long experience for joint probabilities estimated from prohibitively large samples.

Our purpose in this paper is to describe a subjective Bayesian technique that can be used in place of ad hoc scoring functions in rule-based inference systems. Our intent is to retain insofar as possible the well-understood methods of probability theory, introducing only those modifications needed because we are dealing with networks of subjective inference rules [Duda, Hart, and Nilsson 1976 p. 1075].
— Copyright 1976, AFIPS. Reprinted by permission.

8.1.1 Subjective Bayesian Methods

Subjective Bayesian Methods

have the problem

that trial-and-error may be required to tune the probability estimates for acceptable performance.

> The tuning of the Bayesian weights in the inference net was a black art involving guesswork and trial-and-error …. Heuristics exist for the tuning exercise, but there seem to be no hard and fast rules. In particular the tuning is like trying to tune a car with four carburetors—as soon as you have one part right, setting up the next part detunes the first. If the net is tuned to operate reasonably when all the net is in context, then it is guaranteed not to work when parts of the net are out of context [Gasden 1984, p. 90].

8.2 Bidirectional Search

Forward-Chaining combined with Backward-Chaining; that is, Bidirectional Search

has the problem

that unless the two searches intersect properly there may be more effort expended than in a unidirectional search.

> Some problems can be solved using production systems whose rules can be used in either a forward or a backward direction. An interesting possibility is to search in both directions simultaneously. The graph searching process that models such a bidirectional production system can be viewed as one in which search proceeds outward simultaneously from both the start node and from a set of goal nodes. The process terminates when (and if) the two search frontiers meet in some appropriate fashion.
>
> Breadth-first versions of bidirectional graph-searching processes compare favorably with breadth-first unidirectional search.
>
> The situation is more complex, however, when comparing bidirectional and unidirectional *heuristic* searches. If the heuristic functions used by the bidirectional process are even slightly inaccurate, the search frontiers may pass each other without intersecting. In such a case, the bidirectional search process may expand twice as many nodes as would the unidirectional one [Nilsson 1980, p. 88–90].
> — *Principles of Artificial Intelligence* © by Morgan Kaufmann Publishers. Reprinted by permission.

8.3 Blackboards

Blackboards

have the problem

that they may not be the appropriate data structure for all the computation required to solve a given problem.

Remedy: Allow a knowledge source to use whatever special-purpose data structures it needs for its internal processing.

The Hearsay-II approach suggests a very general problem-solving paradigm. Every inference process reads data from the blackboard and places a new hypothesis also on the blackboard. Thus blackboard accesses mediate each decision step. While this proved desirable for structuring communications between different KSs [Knowledge Sources], it proved undesirable for most intermediate decision tasks arising within a single KS. Most KSs employed private, stylized internal data structures different from the single uniform blackboard links and hypotheses. For example, the word recognizer used specialized sequential networks, whereas the word sequence recognizer exploited a large bit-matrix of word adjacencies. Each KS also stored intermediate results, useful for its own internal searches, in appropriately distinctive data structures. Attempts to coerce these specialized activities into the general blackboard-mediated style of Hearsay-II either failed completely or caused intolerable degradation [Lesser and Erman 1977] [Erman, Hayes-Roth, Lesser, and Reddy 1980, p. 246].
  — Copyright 1980, Association for Computing Machinery, Inc. Reprinted by permission.

8.4 Causal Models

Causal Models

have the problem

that the benefits derived may not be worth the expense.

However, while this model [CASNET] uses causal reasoning very effectively, it is not clear that such reasoning is more satisfactory to the end user, or that the physician routinely uses causal reasoning for diagnosis or treatment. The model designer must determine whether one should invest the additional effort necessary to acquire the causal knowledge and represent this knowledge in the computer. The cost/benefit analysis may not be favorable yet for the model designer who is building a practical system. Nor is the design process for causal models as well understood as that for the much simpler production rule models [Weiss and Kulikowski 1984, p. 68].

> — Copyright 1984, Sholom M. Weiss and Casimir A. Kulikowski. Reprinted by permission.

8.5 Chronological Backtracking

Chronological Backtracking

has the problem

that the most recent choice is not necessarily the best one to revise when a dead end is encountered.

Remedy: **Dependency-Directed Backtracking**.

Trial and error can find the right regions but this method of assumed states [i.e., trying out guesses about the unknown state of a device] is potentially combinatorially explosive. ARS [the problem-solving language used by the EL system] supplies dependency-directed backtracking, a scheme which limits the search as follows: The system notes a contradiction when it attempts to solve an impossible algebraic relationship, or when it discovers that a transistor's operating point is not within the possible range for its assumed region. The antecedents of the contradictory facts are scanned to find which nonlinear device state guesses (more generally, the backtrackable choicepoints) are relevant; ARS never tries that combination of guesses again. This is how the justifications (or dependency records) are used to extract and retain more information from each contradiction than a chronological backtracking system. A chronological backtracking system would often have to try many more combinations, each time wasting much labor rediscovering the original contradiction [p. 138].

> — Stallman, R. M., and Sussman, G. J. Forward reasoning and dependency-directed backtracking in a system for computer-aided analysis. *Artificial Intelligence*, *9*, 135–196 (1977). Copyright 1977, Elsevier Science Publishers B.V.

8.6 Confirmation by Exclusion

Confirmation by Exclusion

has the problem

that it is difficult to rule out all the candidate solutions except one when there are many candidates.

Remedy: **Intermediate Hypotheses** that can take the form of **Taxonomies, Causal Networks,** or **Decision Trees.**

By breaking up a large set of candidates into a sequence of decisions, each involving a smaller set of candidates, the opportunities for making effective use of confirmation by exclusion are greatly increased.

> Like the causal graph, a hierarchy of disease categories can be used as a basis for aggregating elements in a differential diagnosis, thereby reducing the apparent number of alternatives to be considered at any one decision point [Pople 1982, pp. 158–159].
> — Pople, H. E., Jr. Heuristic methods for imposing structure on ill-structured problems: The structuring of medical diagnostics. In *Artificial Intelligence in Medicine*, P. Szolovits (ed). Boulder, CO: Westview Press, American Association for the Advancement of Science, 1982, pp. 119–190. Copyright 1982, American Association for the Advancement of Science. Reprinted by permission.

8.7 Constraint Propagation

Constraint Propagation

has the problem

that some applications have complex simulation that outstrip the abilities of algebraic manipulators.

Remedy: Use domain knowledge to identify which variables to solve first.

In order to avoid excessive algebraic manipulation, SYN uses electrical knowledge to guide the manipulations that are done. Propagation of constraints determines which expressions are considered at all. The other source of control SYN has over the algebraic manipulator is the variables it uses in the expressions. The choice of which variables to use, which to solve for, and which to substitute for can affect the amount of resources required to solve a circuit by as much as a factor of ten. The complexity of the algebraic expressions is very sensitive to which unknown quantities are used to express the others. Whenever propagation of constraints gets stuck it introduces a new algebraic variable to break a loop. SYN has considerable latitude to choose which cell in the loop receives the new symbolic quantity. The key declarations in the model definitions suggest good places to break loops. For example, the voltage across r-pi, if known, determines most of the other voltages and currents in a hybrid-pi model of a transistor [de Kleer and Sussman 1980, p. 141].

> — Propagation of constraints applied to circuit synthesis, de Kleer, J., and Sussman, G. J., Copyright 1980. Reprinted by permission of John Wiley & Sons, Ltd.

Constraint Propagation in the service of fault diagnosis

has the problem

that corroboration does not necessarily imply a component is unfaulted.

When two values are equal, we call the coincidence a *corroboration*— when they differ we call it a *conflict*. Coincidences provide information about the assumptions made in the propagation: Corroborations verify them and conflicts indicate at least one of them is in error. This simplistic notion must be substantially adapted before it can be useful in actual troubleshooting.

Its difficulty is that corroborations do not always imply that the components in the derivation are unfaulted. A component should only be considered unfaulted as a consequence of a corroboration if a fault in it would significantly modify its propagated values. This is not, in general, the case. The two most common exceptions occur when the circuit isn't manifesting a symptom or when a particular propagation does not depend significantly on one of its underlying assumptions.

Although a component is faulted, the overall system may still be functioning correctly. (The fault may only manifest itself under certain load conditions, for example.) Therefore a corroboration provides no information if the system is not manifesting a symptom under the specified external conditions (e.g., load and control settings).

The system may be exhibiting a symptom, but the way the faulted component causing the symptom is used in a particular propagation may not be significant. This occurs most commonly when a large quantity is added to a small quantity since the range of the large quantity completely swamps the contribution of the smaller quantity. A similar situation arises when the propagation multiplies an input value by zero [Brown, Burton, and de Kleer 1982, p. 260].
— Copyright 1982, Academic Press. Reprinted by permission.

Constraint Propagation

has the problem

that it does not work well with complex algebraic expressions.

Remedy: **Guess** or **Method of Assumed States**.

The style of analysis performed by EL, which we call *the method of propagation of constraints,* requires the introduction and manipulation of some symbolic quantities. Though the system has routines for symbolic algebra, they can handle only linear relationships. Nonlinear devices such as transistors are represented by piecewise-linear models that cannot be used symbolically; they can be applied only after one has guessed a particular operating region for each nonlinear device in the circuit [p. 138].

Electrical engineering has a method known as the "method of assumed states," which is applicable to piecewise-linear devices such as ideal diodes. It involves making an assumption about which linear region the device is operating in (for a diode, whether it is "on" or "off"). This makes the conditionals simplify away, leaving tractable algebraic expressions to which propagation of constraints applies. Afterwards it is necessary to check that the assumed states are consistent with the voltages and currents that have been determined [p. 147].
— Stallman, R. M., and Sussman, G. J. Forward reasoning and dependency-directed backtracking in a system for computer-aided analysis. *Artificial Intelligence, 9,* 135–196 (1977). Copyright 1977, Elsevier Science Publishers B.V.

Constraint Propagation

has the problem

that sometimes there are no equations that can be solved because there are more unknowns than constraints (equations).

Remedy: **Multiple Views** of the system being modeled if they are available.

In this section and in Section 8.7.1, the quotations use the terminology multiple *models* for Multiple Views.

Parameters in one model may depend upon the behavior of the circuit described by another model. For example, the small signal transconductance of a transistor depends upon the bias current. In design, a desired value of circuit gain may constrain the transconductance. This constraint must eventually be used to constrain the bias current [p. 129].

The resistances of the various resistors appearing in the original circuit appear in the individual models as well. This is another way in which information is shared among the models. Constraints imposed on the aspects of the behavior of the circuit represented by each of these models will combine to constrain the values of the shared parameters. In fact, constructing the bias model caused SYN to refine its view of the gain of the cascode amplifier [p. 131] [de Kleer and Sussman 1980].
— Propagation of constraints applied to circuit synthesis, de Kleer, J., and Sussman, G. J., Copyright 1980. Reprinted by permission of John Wiley & Sons, Ltd.

8.7.1 Multiple Views

Multiple Views

have the problem

that it is difficult to choose the view that is simplest to use for solving the problem.

The incremental model of the cascode amplifier has seven poles! So the transfer function has a seventh degree polynomial in its denominator. This would be awful even if the coefficients were entirely numerical. One source of the complexity is that unnecessarily detailed models are used in the analysis. For example, r_x is often irrelevant; its presence considerably complicates the resulting expressions. If r_x were zero, at least one of those seven poles would go away. We currently have no idea for how to automate the choice of the simplest model appropriate for solving a problem [de Kleer and Sussman 1980, p. 139].
— Propagation of constraints applied to circuit synthesis, de Kleer, J., and Sussman, G. J., Copyright 1980. Reprinted by permission of John Wiley & Sons, Ltd.

8.8   Control Rules

Control Rules

have the problem

that they take time away from working directly on the problem of interest.

MRS differs from PROLOG in that it provides a vocabulary for expressing facts about the process of problem solving and not just about the content. In addition to *content* clauses that describe the application area of a program, we can write *control* clauses in MRS that prescribe how those content clauses are to be used.

The use of control clauses like these can substantially reduce the run time of a logic program. Unfortunately, the overhead of interpreting the control clauses offsets this improvement: For every step of a content-level deduction, the interpreter must complete an entire control-level deduction. In many applications the improved performance is clearly worth the overhead. In others, the overhead swamps the gains, and a simpler interpreter like PROLOG's is preferable [Genesereth and Ginsberg 1985, pp. 938f.].

— Copyright 1985, Association for Computing Machinery, Inc. Reprinted by permission.

Meta-level control, in an Artificial Intelligence system, can provide increased capabilities and improved performance. This improvement, however, is achieved at the cost of the meta-level effort itself. To ensure an overall increase in system efficiency, the savings brought about at the base level cannot be exceeded by the effort at the meta-level [Rosenschein and Singh 1983, p. 1].

Hearsay-II [Blackboard system] uses knowledge interpretively. That is, it actively evaluates alternative actions, chooses the best for the current situation, and then applies the procedure associated with the most promising KS [Knowledge Source] instantiation. Such deliberation takes time and requires many fairly sophisticated mechanisms; its expense can be justified whenever an adequate, explicit algorithm does not exist for the same task. Whenever such an algorithm emerges, equal or greater performance and efficiency may be obtained by compiling the algorithm and executing it directly. For example, recognizing restricted vocabulary and grammatical spoken sentences from limited syntax can now be accomplished faster by techniques other than those in Hearsay-II ..., by compiling all possible interlevel substitutions (sentence to phrase to word to phone to segment) into one enormous finite-state Markov network, the HARPY system uses a modified dynamic programming search to find the one network path that most closely approximates the segmented speech signal. This type of systematic, compiled, and broad search becomes increasingly desirable as problem-solving knowledge improves. Put another way, once a satisfactory specific method for solving any problem is found, the related procedure can be "algorithmetized," compiled, and applied repetitively. In such a case the flexibility of a system like Hearsay-II may no longer be needed [Erman, Hayes-Roth, Lesser, and Reddy 1980, p. 246].

— Copyright 1980, Association for Computing Machinery, Inc. Reprinted by permission.

Control-Rules

have the problem

that they mix badly with exhaustive search. Reordering the search space is rather pointless if the entire space will be searched eventually. Pruning the search space, however, could provide benefits even when all plausible hypotheses will be pursued.

By "meta-rules" the authors of the following quote mean the same technique that we are calling "control-rules." The TEIRESIAS program [Davis 1980] used meta-rules to prune and reorder MYCIN's search for evidence concerning infectious agents.

We have little actual experience with meta-rules in MYCIN, however. Because of the cautious strategy of invoking all relevant rules, we found few opportunities for using them. The one or two meta-rules that made good medical sense could be "compiled out" by moving their contents into the rules themselves. For example, "do rules of type A before those of type B" can be accomplished by manually ordering rules on the UPDATEDBY list or manually ordering clauses in rules. The system overhead of *determining* whether there are any meta-rules to guide rule invocation is a high price to pay if all the rules will be invoked anyway. So, although their potential power for control was demonstrated, their actual utility is being assessed in subsequent ongoing work such as NEOMYCIN [Clancey 1983a] [Buchanan and Shortliffe 1984, p. 679].

— Buchanan/Shortliffe, *Rule-Based Expert Systems*, © 1984 by B. G. Buchanan and E. H. Shortliffe. Reprinted with permission of Addison-Wesley Publishing Co., Inc., Reading, Massachusetts.

8.9 Dempster–Shafer Uncertainty Management

Dempster–Shafer Uncertainty Management

has the problem

that combination of evidence involves an assumption of independence.

The conditional independence of evidence assumed by applications of Bayes Rule is less restrictive than the independence of evidence assumed by Dempster's rule.

> Evidence is accumulated in PSEIKI from both the expected scene information and any internal geometric consistencies that might exist in the image data. Notwithstanding the fact that no single large-scale implementation of any uncertainty formalism exists where researchers did not have to take massive liberties with the underlying assumptions, our use of Dempster's rule is not entirely beyond reproach because we did not address the requirement that evidence sources be independent before being combined. Loosely said, the independence requirement states that the evidence from one source not depend on the evidences from other sources. [Andress and Kak 1988, p. 93].

8.10 EMYCIN Certainty Factors

EMYCIN Certainty Factors

have the problem

that if a number of different rules contribute to the certainty of conclusions, then there is poor ability to discriminate between the amount of support various conclusions receive.

Remedy: Damping Factors; that is, mathematical transformations of the certainty factor scores so that they do not all converge so quickly on 1.

Another limitation for some problems is the rapidity with which CF's [Certainty Factors] converge on the asymptote 1. This is easily seen by plotting the family of curves relating the number of rules with a given CF, all providing evidence for a hypothesis, to the resulting CF associated with the hypothesis.[1] The result of plotting these curves ... is that CF_{COMBINE} is seen to converge rapidly on 1 no matter how small the CF's of the individual rules are. For some problem areas, therefore, the combining function needs to be revised. For example, damping factors of various sorts could be devised (but were not) that would remedy this problem in ways that are meaningful for various domains. In MYCIN's domain of infectious diseases, however, this potential problem never became serious. In PROSPECTOR this problem does not arise because there is no finite upper limit to the likelihood ratios used [Buchanan and Shortliffe 1984, pp. 213–214].

> — Buchanan/Shortliffe, *Rule-Based Expert Systems*, © 1984 by B. G. Buchanan and E. H. Shortliffe. Reprinted with permission of Addison-Wesley Publishing Co., Inc., Reading, Massachusetts.

EMYCIN Certainty Factors

have the problem

that they are only able to reliably separate hypotheses into groups such as "most probable" or "least probable." They are not able to reliably discriminate between the most probable hypotheses to find the best hypothesis because small differences in scores are not meaningful.

Adams [1984] correctly notes that there may be domains where the limitations of the CF [Certainty Factor] model, despite their minimal impact on MYCIN's performance, would seriously constrain the model's applicability and success. For example, if MYCIN had required a single best diagnosis, rather than a clustering of leading hypotheses, there would be reason to doubt the model's ability to select the best hypothesis on the basis of a maximal CF [Buchanan and Shortliffe 1984, p. 214].

> — Buchanan/Shortliffe, *Rule-Based Expert Systems*, © 1984 by B. G. Buchanan and E. H. Shortliffe. Reprinted with permission of Addison-Wesley Publishing Co., Inc., Reading, Massachusetts.

[1]This was first pointed out by Mitch Model, who was investigating the use of the CF model in the context of the HASP/SIAP program [Nii et al., 1982].

8.11   EMYCIN Context Trees

EMYCIN Context Trees

have the problem

that changing the way that the context tree is structured requires large revisions of the expert-system definition.

> Summing up our experience with this mechanism [i.e., EMYCIN context trees] and considering its relative inflexibility, we offer this final caveat: For an initial system design, start small, and use only one or two context types. Plan the structure of your consultant's context tree carefully before running the EMYCIN system, since restructuring a context tree is perhaps the most difficult and time-consuming knowlege-base construction task. Indeed, restructuring the context tree implies a complete restructuring of the rest of the knowledge base [van Melle, Scott, Bennett, and Peairs 1981, p. 21].

EMYCIN Context Trees

have the problem

that they are only designed for homogeneous collections of context instances. If particular instances are distinguished by importance or temporal priority, then it is difficult to give the distinguished instances greater weight in the reasoning.

> ROGET can recommend that the conceptual structure be pruned on several grounds. It inspects the conceptual structure, looking for categories that are notoriously difficult to represent in the system-building tool that was chosen. For example, one such concept that is awkward to represent in EMYCIN is the notion of an important subpart or event. These types of concepts must be represented as contexts in an EMYCIN context tree—a difficult representational mechanism. Reasoning about events and event-progression is very difficult because of the assumed independence of each event instance. In contrast, a category that is easily captured in the EMYCIN framework is the definition of a laboratory test, which can be represented either as a simple context or directly as a set of EMYCIN parameters [Bennett 1985, p. 66].

EMYCIN Context Trees

have the problem

that it is difficult to express relationships between contexts that lie on different branches of the same context tree.

> Reference to parameters of contexts in *different* parts of an instance tree is currently very awkward. For example, in MYCIN, a particular drug may be associated somehow with a particular organism .... However, this relationship between context-instances is *not* one that always holds between all organisms and all drugs: not all drugs are prescribed to treat all identified organisms. This "prescribed for" relationship cannot be stated statically, independently of the case. Special predicate and action functions must be written to establish and manipulate these kinds of relationships between instances. It is best to avoid these interactions between disjoint parts of the tree during the initial design of the knowledge base [Buchanan and Shortliffe 1984, pp. 500f.].
> — Buchanan/Shortliffe, *Rule-Based Expert Systems*, © 1984 by B. G. Buchanan and E. H. Shortliffe. Reprinted with permission of Addison-Wesley Publishing Co., Inc., Reading, Massachusetts.

8.12 Forward-Chaining

Forward-Chaining (i.e., Event-Driven Reasoning)

has the problem

that the inferences can be pointless if they do not contribute to solving the system's goals.

> Advantages of the data-driven approach [Forward-Chaining] include (i) its simplicity and (ii) the fact that it can be used to provide all solutions to a given problem.

> A disadvantage of the data-driven approach is that the behavior of the system, in attempting to solve a problem, can be inefficient and can also appear to be aimless since some of the rules which are executed could be unrelated to the problem at hand [Frost 1986, pp. 427f.].

The following quote comments on an example rule system that involves the Forward-Chaining execution of the abstract rule F & B → Z.

Suppose you had used this system with the express goal of determining whether or not situation Z existed. You might think that it worked quite well, zeroing in quickly on the fact that Z did exist. Unfortunately, this is just an artifact of the example. A real expert system wouldn't have just three rules, it would have hundreds or even thousands of them. If you used a system that large just to find out about Z, many rules would be executed that had nothing to do with Z. A large number of inference chains and situations could be derived that were valid but unrelated to Z. So if your goal is to infer one particular fact, like Z, forward chaining could waste both time and money [Waterman 1986, p. 67].

8.13 Frames

Frames

have the problem

that there is no conventional way to reason with them as there is with rules.

Remedy: Make **Procedural Attachments** do the reasoning (e.g., CENTAUR [Aikins 1980]) or augment with an inference mechanism.

The following quote discusses augmenting a frame system with an inference system.

Recently developed languages for representing knowledge such as KL-ONE [Schmolze and Brachman 1982], Krypton [Brachman, Fikes, and Levesque 1983a], and Nikl [Schmolze and Lipkis 1983], have argued that general frame based languages need to be augmented by a general inferential mechanism. Our embedding FIR in Prolog provides such a mechanism [Finin, McAdams, and Kleinosky 1984, p. 352].
— Copyright 1984 by IEEE.

8.14 Fuzzy-Set Theory

Fuzzy-Set Theory

has the problem

that if the probability of one member of a set of conjuncts is unknown, then the evidence available for the other conjuncts is effectively ignored.

> With logical relations, to compute the probability of a hypothesis from the probability of its component assertions we employ the fuzzy-set formulas of Zadeh [1965]. Using these formulas, the probability of a hypothesis that is defined as the logical conjunction (AND) of several pieces of evidence equals the minimum of the probability values corresponding to the evidence. Similarly, a hypothesis defined as the logical disjunction (OR) of its evidence spaces is assigned a probability value equal to the maximum of those values assigned to the evidence spaces. One property of this procedure is that it often gives no "partial credit." In particular, if all but one of the assertions have been established, but the user can not even guess about the last, then the probability of their conjunction often remains at the value it had when the states of none of the assertions were known [Duda, Gaschnig, and Hart 1979, p. 158].
> — Copyright 1979, Edinburgh University Press. Reprinted by permission.

8.15 Generate-and-Test

Generate-and-Test

has the problem

that the combinatorics of the problem often make it impractical to generate all possible solutions.

Remedy: Use **Hierarchical Generate-and-Test** so only a portion of the solution is generated and then tested. In the best cases, rejecting a partial solution can eliminate the need to generate a large number of candidates. This amounts to pruning a large portion of the search tree. Subsequent Generate-and-Test steps are required to achieve a complete solution.

> In summary, generate-and-test is an appropriate method to consider when it is important to find all solutions to a problem. For the method to be workable, however, the generator must partition the solution space in ways that allow for early pruning. These criteria are often satisfied in data interpretation and diagnostic problems.

There are many problems involving large search spaces for which generate and test is a method of last resort. The most common difficulty is that no generator of solutions can be found for which early pruning is viable. Design and planning problems are of this nature. One usually cannot tell from a fragment of a plan or design whether that fragment is part of a complete solution; there is no reliable evaluator of partial solutions expressed as solution fragments [p. 151].
— Stefik, M., Aikins, J., Balzer, R., Benoit, J., Birnbaum, L., Hayes-Roth, F., and Sacerdoti, E. The organization of expert systems, a tutorial. *Artificial Intelligence, 18*, 135–173 (1982). Copyright 1982, Elsevier Science Publishers B.V.

8.16 Goal-Driven Reasoning

Goal-Driven Reasoning

has the problem

that it is only prepared to make use of items of information when it is working on a goal that requires that information.

The main disadvantage of this control strategy [Goal-Directed Reasoning] is that users cannot interrupt to steer the line of reasoning by volunteering new information. A user can become frustrated, knowing that the system's present line of reasoning will turn out to be fruitless as a result of data that are going to be requested later [Buchanan and Shortliffe 1984, p. 678].
— Buchanan/Shortliffe, *Rule-Based Expert Systems,* © 1984 by B. G. Buchanan and E. H. Shortliffe. Reprinted with permission of Addison-Wesley Publishing Co., Inc., Reading, Massachusetts.

Goal-Driven Reasoning

has the problem

that it is difficult to program the control flow that is required when a set of actions or tests have to be ordered.

Another shortcoming in the formalism arises in part from the backward-chaining control structure. It is not always easy to map a sequence of desired actions or tests into a set of production rules whose goal-directed invocation will provide that sequence. Thus, while the system's performance is reassuringly similar to some human reasoning behavior, the creation of appropriate rules that result in such behavior is at times non-trivial. This may in fact be due more to programming experience that is oriented primarily toward ALGOL-like languages rather than to any essential characteristic of production rules. After some experience with the system we have improved our skill at "thinking backward" [pp. 33–34].

> — Davis, R., Buchanan, B. G., and Shortliffe, E. H. Production rules as a representation for a knowledge-based consultation program. *Artificial Intelligence, 8* (1977). Copyright 1977, Elsevier Science Publishers B.V.

8.17 Inheritance Mechanisms

Inheritance Mechanisms

have the problem

that allowing the overriding or cancelling of default properties makes it difficult to properly represent universal statements (e.g., *All men are mortal*) and definitions (e.g., *A polygon with four sides is a quadrilateral*).

Over the past few years, the notion of a "prototype" (*e.g.,* TYPICAL-ELEPHANT) seems to have caught on securely in knowledge representation research. Along with a way to specify default properties for instances of a description, proto-representations allow the overriding, or "cancelling" of properties that don't apply in particular cases. This supposedly makes representing exceptions (three-legged elephants and the like) easy; but, alas, it makes one crucial type of representation impossible—that of composite descriptions whose meanings are functions of the structure and interrelation of their parts [Brachman 1985, p. 80].

8.18 Intelligent Schedulers

Intelligent Schedulers

(See the Pitfalls described for "Control Rules," above.)

8.19 Least Commitment

Least Commitment

has the problem

that it is hard to keep track of all of the decisions that were deferred and the constraints that the eventual decision must satisfy.

Remedy: **Constraint Posting.**

> In order to refer to an antibiotic without selecting a particular one from the knowledge base, MOLGEN introduces the variable, Antibiotic-1, and posts a pair of constraints to indicate which of the bacteria are supposed to be resistant to it [p. 124].
>
> Constraint-1 states that the bacterium and vector input to the Transform step must be compatible. By posting the constraint, MOLGEN makes the requirement explicit so that it can be combined with the other constraints [p. 121–122].
> — Stefik, M. Planning with constraints (MOLGEN: Part 1). *Artificial Intelligence*, *16*, 111–139 (1981a). Copyright 1981, Elsevier Science Publishers B.V.

Least Commitment

has the problem

of "least commitment deadlock"—when choices need to be made, but no compelling reason exists for deciding on any of them.

Remedy: **Guess.**

> If MOLGEN runs out of things to do (and the plan is incomplete), the plan is said to be under-constrained and it calls upon the Guess operator to make some tentative decision that will enable planning to continue [p. 162].
> — Stefik, M. Planning and meta-planning (MOLGEN: Part 2). *Artificial Intelligence*, *16*, 141–169 (1981b). Copyright 1981, Elsevier Science Publishers B.V.

8.19.1 Guessing

Guessing

has the problem

that it is likely to make the wrong guess or decision and not find the solution.

Remedy: **Chronological Backtracking** or **Dependency-Directed Backtracking**.

8.20 Match

Match

has the problem

that it does not search for solutions.

Remedy: If the problem can be decomposed, then use a search technique for the subproblem that requires it.

It is interesting that Match is in fact insufficient for the complete task in R1. The subtask of placing modules on the UNIBUS is formulated essentially as a bin-packing problem—namely, how to find an optimal sequence that fits within spatial and power constraints. No way of solving this problem without search is known. Consequently R1 uses a different method for this part of the problem [p. 153].
  — Stefik, M., Aikins, J., Balzer, R., Benoit, J., Birnbaum, L., Hayes-Roth, F., and Sacerdoti, E. The organization of expert systems, a tutorial. *Artificial Intelligence*, *18*, 135–173 (1982). Copyright 1982, Elsevier Science Publishers B.V.

8.21 Means–Ends Analysis

Means–Ends Analysis

has the problem

that a table associating operators with differences must be developed for each problem domain.

> In order to use key operators [Means-Ends Analysis], however, the problem solver must be given a procedure for calculating differences and associating key operators with them. A good difference-operator association depends greatly on the problem domain [Nilsson 1971, p. 109].
> — *Problem Solving Methods in Artificial Intelligence* © 1971 by McGraw-Hill. Reprinted by permission.

8.22 Model-Driven Reasoning

Model-Driven Reasoning (also known as Expectation-Driven Reasoning)

has the problem

that the initial hypothesis often turns out to be wrong and the work devoted to it is potentially wasted effort.

Remedy: Store readily confusable hypotheses. This mimics human problem-solvers' use of **Logical Competitor Sets**.

> Because the initial hypotheses are usually generated on the basis of relatively few facts, they will often later prove to be incorrect. In such cases, how does the experienced clinician proceed to undo any "damage" done by aggressive hypothesis generation? Our observations suggest that he or she often employs the rather efficient strategy of associating one hypothesis with others with which it may be readily confused (e.g., "multiple pulmonary emboli are often confused with cardiomyopathy"). By explicitly remembering such situations, the physician can move directly from a hypothesis that has become suspect to one that offers another plausible explanation for the same findings [Pauker, Gorry, Kassirer, and Schwartz 1984, p. 159].

> For the two high-level experts in the study [of pediatric cardiology cases], two distinct methods of using the LCS [Logical Competitor Set] were also identified:

1. *Precaution.* This involves the generation and use *together* as hypotheses of the full set of logical competitors, enabling them to be weighed against each other and the data.

2. *Extraction.* This method involves more aggressive focus on a member of the set, with full expansion to the remainder of the set as disconfirmatory evidence for the target member is found.

Medical students, after six weeks of training and clinical practice in the field represented by the cases, generally showed neither expert form nor expert substance. Students hardly ever considered the full LCS and focused on the "classic" members in cases that encouraged this [Feltovich, Johnson, Moller, and Swanson 1984, p. 311].

8.23 Opportunistic Search

Opportunistic Search

has the problem

that there is no way to know when to stop processing.

Remedy: Specially checked termination conditions or explicit control knowledge.

...There is no prescribed way that the incremental hypothesis formation process terminates short of running out of relevant KSs [Knowledge Sources] [Nii and Aiello 1979, p. 645].

8.24 Partial Matching

Partial Matching

has the problem

that it is inherently expensive in certain worst-case problems.

Remedy: Describe events using the highest-level predicates available.

Because partial-matching subsumes the graph monomorphism, the k-clique, and other NP-complete problems, the amount of time apparently needed to solve worst-case problems is at least exponential in the complexity of the structures being matched. It follows that if partial-matching is to be applied successfully, problem complexity must be reduced. The principal way in which such complexity reduction can be accomplished is by choosing rich, high-order predicates as a basis for description. As the grain of description is reduced toward uniform, low-level predicates (e.g., simple graphs, retinal arrays of on–off detectors, semantic primitives), the partial-matching problem is made inherently more complex and less feasible [Hayes-Roth 1978, p. 570].
— Copyright 1978, Academic Press. Reprinted by permission.

Partial Matching

has the problem

that it often finds more than one best match.

Any partial-matching problem can produce a large number of alternative solutions of varying plausibility [Hayes-Roth 1978, p. 570].
— Copyright 1978, Academic Press. Reprinted by permission.

8.25 Resolution

Resolution

has the problem

that it can be inefficient.

Remedy: **Linear Input Strategy** or some other restriction of general resolution.

If resolution were applied without guidance, it would produce numerous useless propositions. To mitigate this problem, DART draws only those conclusions in which at least one of the resolvents is an assertion in the design model. No resolutions are performed between conclusions and other conclusions. This restriction is often called the "linear input strategy" [Nilsson 1980] and is very effective in preventing an undesirable proliferation of useless conclusions [Genesereth 1982, p. 282].

8.26 Rules

Rules

have the problem

that incompatible rules may be potentially applicable at the same time.

Remedy: **Conflict-Resolution Strategies** [McDermott, J. and Forgy 1978], or apply all the rules whose left-hand sides are satisfied, and when the rule firings stop, compare the amount of evidence that has accumulated for each hypothesis.

8.27 Scoring Functions

Scoring Functions

have the problem

that they can focus on the wrong hypothesis if they are too sensitive to the amount of data and not sensitive enough to the importance of the data.

The scoring mechanism does not always lead to an appropriate task definition, however, as the procedure can be sensitive to the preponderance of data as well as the more relevant measures of specificity and importance. Thus it sometimes happens that important, specific data are "disregarded" by INTERNIST's problem-focusing heuristic while less significant facts of the clinical problem are selected for investigation on the basis of a large volume of data, much of which might be of limited importance [Pople 1982, p. 147].
> — Pople, H. E., Jr. Heuristic methods for imposing structure on ill-structured problems: The structuring of medical diagnostics. In *Artificial Intelligence in Medicine*, P. Szolovits (ed). Boulder, CO: Westview Press, American Association for the Advancement of Science, 1982, pp. 119–190. Copyright 1982, American Association for the Advancement of Science. Reprinted by permission.

Scoring Functions

have the problem

that they make it difficult to generate lines of reasoning that parallel those of clinical experts.

> When several top-ranking hypotheses have scores that are close in value, reflecting a very ambiguous case, the interpretation of additional data may often result in rapid changes in the focus of reasoning, as one piece of evidence pushes the score of one hypothesis above that of its competitors, and then another finding elevates the score of an alternative hypothesis above that of the first. To avoid an overdependence on scoring functions, all AIM [Artificial Intelligence in Medicine] systems have tried to incorporate into their knowledge bases as many categorical reasoning links as possible [Kulikowski 1980, p. 471].
> — Copyright 1980 by IEEE.

> To its user, PIP's reasoning is discernible from the conclusions it reaches and the focus of its questioning. PIP appears unnatural when its focus frequently shifts, as the probabilistic evaluator brings first one and then another competing hypothesis to the fore. This major deficiency relates to the lack of categorical reasoning. Such reasoning might impose a longer-term discipline or diagnostic style [Miller 1975] on the diagnostic process [p. 128].
> — Szolovits, P., and Pauker, S. G. Categorical and probabilistic reasoning in medical diagnosis. *Artificial Intelligence, 11,* 115–144 (1978). Copyright 1978, Elsevier Science Publishers B.V.

8.28 Semantic Networks

Semantic Networks

have the problem

that only unary and binary predicates are easily expressed.

Remedy: Introduce an object that stands for any predication that has more than two arguments.

> Turning now to semantic networks, a first observation about a KB [Knowledge Base] in this form is that it only contains unary and binary predicates. For example, instead of representing the fact that John's grade in cs100 was 85 by

$$Grade(john, cs100, 85)$$

we would postulate the existence of objects called "grade-assignments" and represent the fact about John in terms of a particular grade assignment e as

Grade-assignment(e) $\wedge$ Student(e, john) $\wedge$ Course(e, cs100) $\wedge$ Mark(e, 85)

[Levesque 1984, p. 148].

> — Levesque, H. J. A fundamental tradeoff in knowledge representation and reasoning. *Proceedings of the Fourth Conference of the Canadian Society for Computational Studies of Intelligence*, London, Ontario, 1984, pp. 141–152. Copyright 1984, Canadian Society for Computational Studies of Intelligence. Reprinted by permission.

Semantic Networks

have the problem

that they have a number of shortcomings in expressive power.

Moreover, I hope that I have made the point that when one does extract a clear understanding of the semantics of the notation, most of the existing semantic network notations are found wanting in some major respects—notably the representation of propositions without commitment to asserting their truth and in representing various types of intensional descriptions of objects without commitment to their external existence, their external distinctness, or their completeness in covering all of the objects which are presumed to exist in the world. I have also pointed out the logical inadequacies of almost all current network notations for representing quantified information and some of the disadvantages of some logically adequate techniques.

I have not begun to address all of the problems that need to be addressed, and I have only begun to discuss the problems of relative clauses and quantificational information. I have not even mentioned other problems such as the representation of mass terms, adverbial modification, probabilistic information, degrees of certainty, time, and tense, and a host of other difficult problems. All of these issues need to be addressed and solutions integrated into a consistent whole in order to produce a logically adequate semantic network formalism. No existing semantic network comes close to this goal [Woods 1975, p. 80].

> — Copyright 1975, Academic Press. Reprinted by permission.

Semantic Networks

have the problem

that they are unable to express some of the standard logical connectives.

Remedy: **Partitioned Semantic Networks.**

A representation scheme for negations, disjunctions, and implications must allow one or more "worlds" to be described and a relationship to be asserted among the worlds (e.g., that at least one of them is true). K-NET's partitioning facilities provide the required capabilities for creating just such a scheme [Fikes and Hendrix 1977, p. 237].

8.29 Truth Maintenance Systems

Truth Maintenance Systems

have the problem

that it is difficult to compare alternative solutions because only one consistent set of choices can be considered at a time.

Remedy: **Assumption-Based Truth Maintenance Systems.**

Given a set of choices which admits multiple solutions, the TMS [Truth Maintenance System] algorithms only allow one solution to be considered at a time. This makes it extremely difficult to compare equally plausible solutions. For example, suppose A,D,E,G and B,C,E,G are both solutions. It is impossible to examine both of these states simultaneously. However, this is often exactly what one wants to do in problem solving—differential diagnosis to determine the best solution.

The assumption-based scheme allows arbitrarily many contradictory solutions to coexist. Thus it is simple to compare two solutions [de Kleer 1984, pp. 81f.].
> — Reprinted with permission from *Proceedings of the National Conference on Artificial Intelligence*, 1984, pp. 81f., published by the American Association for Artificial Intelligence.

The ATMS [Assumption-Based Truth Maintenance System] is not a panacea and is not suited to all tasks. Conventional TMS's are oriented to finding one solution, and extra cost is incurred to control the TMS to find many solutions. The ATMS is oriented to finding all solutions, and extra cost is incurred to control the ATMS to find fewer solutions [p. 137].

   — de Kleer, J. An assumption-based TMS. *Artificial Intelligence*, *28*, 127–162 (1986). Copyright 1986, Elsevier Science Publishers B.V.

9 Future Applications of Design Guidelines

R9 If the search space is moderately small,
   then exhaustive search is feasible.

... the same metarule, R9, has been used in three distinct roles: to aid in designing a system, to aid in knowing when and how to redesign a system, and to answer "why" questions of a fundamental nature.

[Lenat, Davis, Doyle, Genesereth, Goldstein, and Shrobe 1983, p. 232].

A number of expert-system building tools or shells are available today, for example, EMYCIN, Personal Consultant[TM], KEE[R], ART[R], and KnowledgeCraft[TM]. Each of these programming environments provides convenient access to some subset of the AI implementation techniques recommended by the design guidelines of this book. We expect that future programming environments for building expert systems will explicitly incorporate design guidelines as well as implementation techniques. As the quote at the beginning of this chapter suggests, there are at least three roles that design guidelines could play if they were incorporated in programming environments: initial design assistance, recommendations for redesign, and answering certain questions asked by users of the expert system.

9.1 INITIAL DESIGN ASSISTANCE

Building design guidelines into an expert-system tool would make it possible to go beyond just saying "Your problem sounds like one that would lend itself to Frames." By conducting a dialogue with the expert-system builder, an expert-system tool with knowledge of the design guidelines in this book could determine that Frames appear to be appropriate for a particular problem. The next step would be to direct the expert-system builder to the Frame Builder interface if the tool has one, or at least to direct that person toward the proper LISP functions if that is the best it can do. Using the guidelines to provide design assistance tailored to a particular expert-system programming environment would go a long way toward making the advice offered by these guidelines operational.

Most of the existing expert-system tools support only a small subset of the techniques that are recommended in this book. Since users of these programming environments do not have access to all these techniques, is there anything to be gained by considering all these guidelines? One reason for considering the entire set of guidelines is that guidelines recommending unsupported techniques are likely to identify problem features that will present implementation obstacles. It should be valuable to point out these potential obstacles to users and, if possible, advise them as to how those difficulties are generally overcome with the techniques that are supported.

Several existing programs know enough about designing expert systems within the context of a particular programming environment to begin to assist users in building their own expert systems. For example, the ROGET program [Bennett 1984, 1985] knows how to design portions of an expert system within the EMYCIN programming environment. The MORE program [Kahn, Nowlan, and McDermott 1984; Kahn 1988] knows how to design portions of a expert system using the programming environment developed to build the MUD system.

The EMYCIN program is one particular choice of an expert-system design and so is MUD. Therefore, the role of ROGET and MORE is not to assist in developing an expert-system design, but rather to assist in knowledge acquisition within the confines of one particular design. Of course, the fact that ROGET and MORE can assume a detailed architecture for the target expert system pays dividends in that they can offer quite detailed advice. The breadth of advice provided by the guidelines presented in this book would pay dividends in a more general-purpose programming environment where the selection of different components allows the construction of expert systems with significantly different designs.

9.2 SUBOPTIMAL USE OF TECHNIQUES OR NEED FOR REDESIGN

A programming environment that has a knowledge base containing the guidelines presented in this book is in a position to understand the reasons for the use of a particular AI implementation technique. This knowledge makes it possible for that programming environment to assist programmers by pointing out that the use of a technique fails, in certain respects, to achieve the objectives that motivated the use of that technique.

For example, when object-oriented programming has been adopted, it defeats the purpose of sharing common capabilities and behaviors (see Guideline 7.5) to create an object that only has one descendant inheriting its capabilities. The programming environment could actively look for objects with single descendants and when it finds one, point out to the programmer that it would be more straightforward to eliminate the ancestor object and attach all its capabilities to the descendant.

This monitoring should take place not only during the initial creation of the expert system but also during modification and update stages. A single-ancestor situation will often arise during modifications without the programmer even being aware of it. For example, single descendants often arise as the unintended by-product of the elimination of descendants, rather than the deliberate creation of a single descendant.

Many of the guidelines presented in this book could be used to generate monitors or demons to look for situations that potentially compromise the usefulness of a technique or design decision. We offer a few other suggestions of monitors that would be useful to include in an expert-system programming environment:

1. If the expert system is using Chronological Backtracking, then determine whether the amount of system resources being consumed by backtracking makes it worthwhile to implement Dependency-Directed Backtracking (see Section 8.5).
2. If the expert system is using Control Rules, then monitor the agenda to determine whether all the entries are eventually executed anyway. Such a finding would suggest that little is being gained from the Control Rules (see Guideline 5.1 and Section 8.8).

3. The programming environment should try to determine certain properties of the search spaces that are typically encountered. For example, is the search space "bushier" in one direction or in the other? Are there "bottlenecks" or critical paths? If so, it should recommend searching in the direction that avoids the high branching parts of the search space or Means–Ends Analysis to efficiently achieve the critical path (see Guideline 2.9).

4. If the expert system is using Forward-Chaining, check whether many of the inferences are fruitless in the sense that no use is made of the new assertions (see Section 8.12).

5. If the expert system is using a combination of Forward- and Backward-Chaining, the programming environment should look for evidence that the forward and backward searches are failing to link up. Failure to link up leads to a duplication of effort (see Section 8.2).

6. The programming environment should recommend replacing dynamically determined decisions with hard-wired selections whenever the monitors can detect patterns that make it possible to predict the outcome of those decisions in advance (see Section 8.8).

7. If a cost–benefit analysis is being performed to decide on the best information to gather (see Guideline 5.2) or the best line of reasoning to pursue (see Guideline 5.1), then the system could try to validate the estimates of costs and benefits in terms of actual experience on problems.

Rather than simply telling programmers that they might want to consider changing the implementation, in certain selected cases the programming environment might want to volunteer to change the implementation itself whenever the change is sufficiently straightforward. Ideas along these lines (motivated more by efficiency considerations than design considerations) have been proposed under the label of "cognitive economy" by Lenat, Hayes-Roth, and Klahr [1979].

9.3 RESPONSE TO USER QUERIES

The third advantage to incorporating design guidelines in an expert-system programming environment is the ability they provide to answer certain user questions. For example, Lenat, Davis, Doyle, Genesereth, Goldstein, and Shrobe [1983, p. 232] discuss the scenario where the user asks why the system is pursuing such an unlikely hypothesis. The system responds by saying that it is performing an exhaustive search of all the hypotheses. If at this point the user goes on to ask why an exhaustive search, then Lenat et al. argue that their design guideline R9 provides the appropriate answer:

> R9 If the search space is moderately small,
>
> then exhaustive search is feasible.

The same point can be made using some of the guidelines from this book. For example, a user might ask why the expert system is interested in collecting evidence that is aimed at ruling candidates out as opposed to collecting evidence aimed at ruling candidates in. Guidelines 2.4 and 2.1, can be used to explain the use of Generate-and-Test and Confirmation by Exclusion.

A user might also wonder why an expert system doing data interpretation concentrates on items in the middle of a data sequence as opposed to proceeding systematically through the data elements from beginning to end. In this case Guideline 3.3 could be used to explain the use of Island-Driving as a way of using the most clear cut parts of the data to help interpret the more difficult parts of the data.

9.4 CONCLUSION

This book has presented a number of design guidelines for building expert systems. Since the field of expert systems is still in its infancy, the guidelines that have been assembled are almost certainly inadequate in some respects. The hope is that they will be valuable to expert-system builders despite their inadequacies. Even an imperfect set of design guidelines can provide major benefits by allowing designers to explore the promise of this new technology.

It is worth considering what might help produce a more adequate set of design guidelines. One observation is that there is no real shortage of claims linking AI techniques to problem characteristics. The large number of quotations reproduced in this book provides one demonstration of that fact. However, there is a shortage of *dialogue* about these claims. Expert-system builders make whatever claims they wish for the applicability of their techniques without fear of contradiction. Little or no attention is paid to the claims that have been made by other authors.

The issue of what problem characteristics render an AI technique appropriate is certainly important enough to disagree about. Hopefully, in the future this issue will receive the benefit of vigorous debate. Perhaps exhibiting some of these claims in this book will draw attention to them and help stimulate such a debate.

APPENDIX A

Glossary

AGENDA

A prioritized list of pending activities, usually the applications of various
pieces of knowledge [Hayes-Roth, Waterman and Lenat, 1983, p. 399].
— Hayes-Roth/Waterman/Lenat, *Building Expert Systems,* © 1983, Addison-
Wesley Publishing Co., Inc., Reading, Massachusetts. Reprinted with permission.

ASSERTIONS

An assertion is a statement of fact that is always true. The following
quote explains how to express an assertion in PROLOG.

A Horn clause with a conclusion, but no condition, is called an <u>assertion</u>
[p. 29].
— Reprinted by permission of the publisher from *Logic for Problem Solving*
by R. Kowalski. Copyright 1979 by Elsevier Science Publishing Co., Inc.

ASSUMPTION-BASED TRUTH MAINTENANCE
SYSTEM

My solution is to include with each assertion, in addition to its justifications, the set of choices (assumptions) under which it holds. For example,

each assertion derived from assumption A is labeled with the set $\{A\}$, each assertion derived from both assumptions A and B is labeled with the set $\{A,B\}$. Thus if $x = 1$ under assumption A and $x + y = 0$ under assumption B then we deduce $y = -1$ under assumption set $\{A,B\}$. ... Unlike a TMS [Truth Maintenance System] where the same node can be brought in and out an arbitrary number of times, a value is removed from the data base only if its assumption set is found to be contradictory. For example, the database can contain both $\langle x = 1, \{A\}, \rangle$ and $\langle x = 0, \{B\}, \rangle$ without difficulty. ... As this scheme is primarily based on assumptions, not justifications I term it *assumption-based* as opposed to *justification-based* TMS systems. [de Kleer 1984].
  — Reprinted with permission from *Proceedings of the National Conference on Artificial Intelligence*, 1984, p. 81f., published by the American Association for Artificial Intelligence.

BACKWARD-CHAINING

MYCIN primarily uses backward chaining, or a goal-directed control strategy. ... In goal-directed reasoning a system starts with a statement of the goal to achieve and works "backward" through inference rules, i.e., from right to left, to find the data that establish that goal, for example:

Find out about C	(Goal)
If B, then C	(Rule 1)
<u>If A, then B</u>	(Rule 2)
$\therefore$ If A, then C	(Implicit Rule)
Question: Is A true?	(Data)

[Buchanan and Shortliffe 1984, p. 5].
  — Buchanan/Shortliffe, *Rule-Based Expert Systems*, © 1984 by B. G. Buchanan and E. H. Shortliffe. Reprinted with permission of Addison-Wesley Publishing Co., Inc., Reading, Massachusetts.

BAYES RULE

Bayes Rule is expressed as follows:

$$P(H \mid E) = \frac{P(E \mid H)P(H)}{P(E)},$$

where H is a hypothesis, E is a piece of evidence, $P(H \mid E)$ is the probability of H given that E is observed, $P(E \mid H)$ is the probability of E given that H is true, $P(H)$ is the *a priori* probability of H, and $P(E)$ is the *a priori* probability of E.

BLACKBOARD

A globally accessible data base used in HEARSAY-II and other systems for recording intermediate, partial results of problem-solving. Typically, the blackboard is partitioned for representing hypotheses at different levels of abstraction and mediates activities of multiple "subexperts" or specialists [Hayes-Roth, Waterman, and Lenat 1983, p. 399].

> — Hayes-Roth/Waterman/Lenat, *Building Expert Systems*, © 1983, Addison-Wesley Publishing Co., Inc., Reading, Massachusetts. Reprinted with permission.

The blackboard model is usually described as consisting of three major components ... :

The knowledge sources. The knowledge needed to solve the problem is partitioned into *knowledge sources*, which are kept separate and independent.

The blackboard data structure. The problem-solving state data are kept in a global database, the *blackboard*. Knowledge sources produce changes to the blackboard that lead incrementally to a solution to the problem. Communication and interaction among the knowledge sources take place solely through the blackboard.

Control. The knowledge sources respond opportunistically to changes in the blackboard.[1]

[Nii 1986, p. 39].

> — Reprinted with permission from *AI Magazine*, 1986, p. 39, published by the American Association for Artificial Intelligence.

BREADTH-FIRST SEARCH

The breadth-first method expands nodes in order of their proximity to the start node, measured by the number of arcs between them. In other words, it considers every possible operator sequence of length n before

---

[1]There is no control component specified in the blackboard model. The model merely specifies a general problem-solving behavior. The actual locus of control can be in the knowledge sources, on the blackboard, in a separate module, or in some combination of the three.

any sequence of length $n + 1$. Thus, although the search may be an extremely long one, it is guaranteed eventually to find the shortest possible solution sequence if any solution exists [Barr and Feigenbaum 1981, p. 47].

CAUSAL MODELS

The following quote describes three types of systems that apply knowledge regarding causal relationships. When we refer to causal models in this book, we have in mind either a mediated or a dynamic system in Kahn's terms.

For purposes of discussion, the evidential to causal continuum can be more sharply segmented into

- **Compiled** evidential systems in which the relation between a hypothesis and a set of evidential considerations is explicitly represented and a hypothesis is confirmed if a support function over the evidence returns a high enough value.

- **Mediated** systems in which top level symptoms are linked stepwise via evidential considerations to a set of proximal causes which in turn, as the consequences of other events, chain back to a distal event that the system will select as an explanatory cause; and

- **Dynamic** systems in which a model is manipulated until it appears to simulate the behavior of the real system for which a diagnosis is required.

[pp. 22–23].
  — Kahn, G. On when diagnostic systems want to do without causal knowledge. In *ECAI-84: Advances in Artificial Intelligence*, T. O'Shea (ed.). Amsterdam: Elsevier, 1984, pp. 21–30. Copyright 1984, Elsevier Science Publishers B.V.

CHRONOLOGICAL BACKTRACKING

A search procedure that makes guesses at various points during problem-solving and returning to a previous point to make another choice when a guess leads to an unacceptable result [Hayes-Roth, Waterman, and Lenat 1983, p. 399].

CONDITIONAL INDEPENDENCE

A second assumption often made is that test results are conditionally independent—i.e., given that some hypothesis is the true state of the world, the probability of observing result $R_{i,k}$ for test T_i does not depend on what results have been obtained for any other test.

In a small study of the diagnosis of left-sided valvular heart disease, we have found that assuming conditional independence between observations of systolic and diastolic heart murmurs leads (not surprisingly) to erroneously reversed conclusions from those obtained by a proper analysis. To the extent that anatomical and physiological mechanisms tie together many of the observations that we can make of the patient's condition and to the extent that our probabilistic models are incapable of capturing those ties, simplifications in the computational model will lead to errors of diagnosis [pp. 216–217].
— Szolovits, P., and Pauker, S. G. Categorical and probabilistic reasoning in medical diagnosis. *Artificial Intelligence*, *11*, 115–144 (1978). Copyright 1978, Elsevier Science Publishers B.V.

CONFIRMATION BY EXCLUSION

It is an old maxim of mine that when you have excluded the impossible, whatever remains, however improbable, must be the truth [Conan Doyle, 1892].

CONFLICT-RESOLUTION STRATEGIES

Conflict resolution is the process of determining which rules to execute when more than one rule is applicable. One of the goals of conflict resolution is to select a rule on the basis of global considerations, which are unknown to each of the relevant production rules. For example, the R1 expert system relies on the *special-case* conflict-resolution strategy:

Given two instantiations, one of which contains a proper subset of the data elements contained by the other, OPS4 will select the instantiation containing more data elements on the assumption that it is specialized for the particular situation at hand [McDermott, J. 1982, pp. 45f.].

Other examples of conflict-resolution strategies are given in McDermott and Forgy [1978].

CONSTRAINT POSTING

The MOLGEN program formulates and represents a constraint before it attempts to find values for variables that satisfy that constraint.

> Instead of choosing values for the variables, it [MOLGEN] formulates a constraint on their values that can be taken into account in a later constraint satisfaction step. *Constraint-1* states that the bacterium and vector input to the **Transform** step must be compatible. By posting the constraint, MOLGEN makes the requirement explicit so that it can be combined with other constraints [p. 121–122].
> — Stefik, M. Planning with constraints (MOLGEN: Part 1). *Artificial Intelligence*, *16*, 111–139 (1981a). Copyright 1981, Elsevier Science Publishers B.V.

CONSTRAINT PROPAGATION

> In general a constraint propagation system has a set of "cells" which can take on values, and a set of "constraints" which constrain those values. Whenever a new value follows from the previously determined values and a *single* constraint, this value is deduced. In what will be termed "simple" constraint propagation these are the only deductions which are made. Constraint propagation terminates when there are no further deductions which can be made from single constraints [McAllester 1980, p. 2].
> — Copyright 1980, Massachusetts Institute of Technology. Reprinted by permission.

CONSTRAINT RELAXATION

> One of the first issues to be faced in the representation of constraints is *conflict*. Consider cost and due-date constraints, the former may require reduction of costs while the latter may require shipping the order in a short period of time. To accomplish the latter may require using faster, more expensive machines, hence conflicting with the former. If the conflict cannot be solved, one or both constraints must "give ground" or be *relaxed*. This is implicitly accomplished in mathematical programming

and decision theory by means of utility functions and the specifications of relaxation through bounds on a variable's value. In AI, bounds on a variable are usually specified by predicates [Stefik 1981a; Engleman, Scarl, and Berg 1980] or choice sets [Steele 1980, Waltz 1975]. In ISIS, our objective is to extend the general representation of knowledge to include the specification of constraints and their relaxations [p. 7].

— Reprinted with permission from Fox, M. S. *Constraint-Directed Search: A Case Study of Job-Shop Scheduling.* CMU-RI-TR-83-22, The Robotics Institute, Carnegie-Mellon University 1983.

DATA ABSTRACTION

For many problems, solution features are not supplied as data, but are inferred by *data abstraction*. There are three basic relations for abstracting data in heuristic programs:

(1) *definitional abstraction* based on essential, necessary features of a concept ("if the structure is a one-dimensional network, then its shape is a beam");

(2) *qualitative abstraction*, a form of definition involving quantitative data, usually with respect to some normal or expected value ("if the patient is an adult and white blood count is less than 2500, then the white blood count is low"); and

(3) *generalization* in a subtype hierarchy ("if the client is a judge, then he is an educated person").

These interpretations are usually made by the program with certainty; belief thresholds and qualifying conditions are chosen so the abstraction is categorical. It is common to refer to this knowledge as being 'factual' or 'definitional' [Clancey 1985, p. 294].

DATA-DRIVEN REASONING

By *data-driven* we mean "inferred from the input data" [Nii, Feigenbaum, Anton, and Rockmore 1982].

— Reprinted with permission from *AI Magazine*, 1982, p. 35, published by the American Association for Artificial Intelligence.

DECISION TREE

A tree-structured network encoding a set of tests to classify a collection of objects (also situations and events) into fixed categories according to predetermined features of the objects.

DEMPSTER–SHAFER THEORY

An uncertainty management theory that distinguises between upper and lower bounds on probabilities and where probability can be assigned to sets of hypotheses as well as individual hypotheses. See Gordon and Shortliffe [1985] for a definition and ideas on how to apply the theory to medical diagnosis.

DEPENDENCY-DIRECTED BACKTRACKING

An alternative to **chronological backtracking** where the backtrack point (the choice point that control is passed back to on failure) is determined by the nature of the failure. That is, the choice that caused the failure is undone whereas in chronological backtracking it is simply the last choice that is reconsidered. Some of the work done since the faulty choice may be independent of that choice, and with appropriate techniques much of this work can be retained [Bundy 1984, p. 28].
— Copyright 1984, Springer-Verlag Heidelberg. Reprinted by permission.

DEPTH-FIRST SEARCH

In depth-first methods we expand the most recently generated nodes first. We define the depth of a node in a tree as follows:

> The depth of the root is zero
>
> The depth of any node that is a descendent of the root
>
> is one plus the depth of its parent

Thus the currently deepest node in the search tree is the one selected for expansion [Nilsson 1971, pp. 48–49].
— *Problem Solving Methods in Artificial Intelligence* © 1971 by McGraw-Hill. Reprinted by permission.

DIVIDE-AND-CONQUER

Given a function to compute on n inputs the *divide-and-conquer* strategy suggests splitting the inputs into k distinct subsets, $1 < k \leq n$ yielding k subproblems. These subproblems must be solved and then a method must be found to combine subsolutions into a solution of the whole. If the subproblems are still relatively large, then the divide-and-conquer strategy may possibly be reapplied. Often the subproblems resulting from a divide-and-conquer design are of the *same* type as the original problem. For those cases the reapplication of the divide-and-conquer principle is naturally expressed by a recursive procedure. Now smaller and smaller subproblems of the same kind are generated, eventually producing subproblems that are small enough to be solved without splitting [Horowitz and Sahni 1978, p. 98].

EMYCIN CERTAINTY FACTORS

Since we want to deal with real-world domains in which reasoning is often judgmental and inexact, we require some mechanism for being able to say "*A suggests B*" or "*C* and *D tend* to rule out *E*." The numbers used to indicate the strength of a rule...have been termed Certainty Factors (CFs). The methods for combining CFs are embodied in a model of approximate implication. Note that while these are derived from and are related to probabilities, they are distinctly different (for a detailed review of the concept, see Shortliffe and Buchanan [1975]). ...Evidence confirming a hypothesis is collected separately from that disconfirming it, and the truth of a hypothesis at any time is the algebraic sum of the current evidence for and against it. This is an important aspect of the truth model, since it makes plausible the simultaneous existence of evidence in favor of and against the same hypothesis. We believe this is an important characteristic of any model of inexact reasoning [p. 22].
   — Davis, R., Buchanan, B. G., and Shortliffe, E. H. Production rules as a representation for a knowledge-based consultation program. *Artificial Intelligence, 8* (1977). Copyright 1977 Elsevier Science Publishers B.V.

EXHAUSTIVE SEARCH

Exhaustive Search means exploring the entire search space.

The absence of complete certainty in most of our [MYCIN] rules meant that we needed a control structure that would consider *all* rules regarding a given hypothesis and not stop after the first one had succeeded. This

need for exhaustive search was distinctly different from control in DEN-DRAL where the hierarchical ordering of rules was particularly important for correct prediction and interpretation [Buchanan and Shortliffe 1984, p. 56].
— Buchanan/Shortliffe, *Rule-Based Expert Systems*, © 1984 by B. G. Buchanan and E. H. Shortliffe. Reprinted with permission of Addison-Wesley Publishing Co., Inc., Reading, Massachusetts.

EXPECTATION-DRIVEN REASONING

A control procedure that employs current data and decisions to formulate hypotheses about yet unobserved events and to allocate resources to activities that confirm, disconfirm, or monitor the expected events [Hayes-Roth, Waterman, and Lenat 1983, p. 400].
— Hayes-Roth/Waterman/Lenat, *Building Expert Systems*, © 1983, Addison-Wesley Publishing Co., Inc., Reading, Massachusetts. Reprinted with permission.

EXPERT SYSTEM

A computer system that achieves high levels of performance in task areas that, for human beings, require years of special education and training [Hayes-Roth, Waterman, and Lenat 1983, p. 400].
— Hayes-Roth/Waterman/Lenat, *Building Expert Systems*, © 1983, Addison-Wesley Publishing Co., Inc., Reading, Massachusetts. Reprinted with permission.

One virtue of this definition is that it rules out vision systems and natural-language systems because they do not address tasks that humans need years of special education to acquire. Chess programs that rely on rapid, brute-force search rather than deep knowledge about chess should probably be ruled out, too, and this leads to the further requirement that the expert system and the human experts achieve their high levels of performance on the basis of roughly the same knowledge. (Ruling out vision systems and similar systems from the definition is useful because it keeps the term "expert system" from becoming synonymous with "AI system.")

FIRST-ORDER LOGIC

See "Predicate Calculus."

FORWARD-CHAINING

The inference mechanism can take many forms. We often speak of the control structure or control of inference to reflect the fact that there are different controlling strategies for the system. For example, a set of rules may be chained together, as in this example:

> If A, then B   (Rule 1)
>
> If B, then C   (Rule 2)
>
> <u>A   </u>   (Data)
>
> $\therefore$ C   (Conclusion)

This is sometimes called forward chaining, or data-directed inference, because the data that are known (in this case A) drive the inferences from left to right in rules, with rules chaining together to deduce a conclusion (C) [Buchanan and Shortliffe 1984, pp. 4f.].
— Buchanan/Shortliffe, *Rule-Based Expert Systems,* © 1984 by B. G. Buchanan and E. H. Shortliffe. Reprinted with permission of Addison-Wesley Publishing Co., Inc., Reading, Massachusetts.

FRAMES

A knowledge representation scheme that associates one or more features with an object in terms of various *slots* and particular *slot-values.* Similar to *property-list, schema, unit,* and *record* in various writings [Hayes-Roth, Waterman, and Lenat 1983, p. 400].
— Hayes-Roth/Waterman/Lenat, *Building Expert Systems,* © 1983, Addison-Wesley Publishing Co., Inc., Reading, Massachusetts. Reprinted with permission.

A *frame* is a data-structure for representing a stereotyped situation, like being in a certain kind of living room, or going to a child's birthday party.

We can think of a frame as a network of nodes and relations. The "top levels" of a frame are fixed, and represent things that are always true about the supposed situation. The lower levels have many *terminals*— "slots" that must be filled by specific instances or data. Each terminal can specify conditions its assignments must meet. (The assignments themselves are usually smaller "subframes.") Simple conditions are specified by markers that might require a terminal assignment to be a person, an object of sufficient value, or a pointer to a sub-frame of a certain type. More complex conditions can specify relations among the things assigned to several terminals [Minsky 1975, p. 212].

— *The Psychology of Computer Vision* © 1975 by McGraw-Hill. Reprinted by permission.

FUZZY-SET THEORY

Most heuristic methods have sought to justify their approach by some quasi-probabilistic interpretation. Yet there are other logical formalisms within which the reasoning of experts can be described. One such formalism is *fuzzy logic*, which uses a multi-valued *membership function* to denote membership of an object in a class rather than the classical binary *true* or *false* values of Boolean logic. Thus, a person will not be considered to be either old or young, but, depending on his actual age, can have certain degree of being old, and a different degree of being young, both of which will depend on the membership functions that people define for the concepts of *old* and *young*. If we take a fuzzy logic approach, we handle conjunctions by using the minimum weight to attach to the whole LHS [left-hand side of a rule] [Weiss and Kulikowski 1984, p. 39].

— Copyright 1984, Sholom M. Weiss and Casimir A. Kulikowski. Reprinted by permission.

GENERATE-AND-TEST

A problem-solving method. A generator process outputs solution candidates one at a time. A test process then accepts or rejects them. In classical Generate-and-Test the generator outputs full-blown solution candidates, say the entire seven digit combination of a safe. A variant that has been identified is **Hierarchical Generate-and-Test**, where only a portion of the solution is generated and then tested. Subsequent Generate-and-Test steps are required to achieve a complete solution. An example is DENDRAL, which generates partial molecules and tests them against the available data before extending the candidate molecule. When the problem can be factored into steps in this way, there are efficiency advantages over one-shot Generate-and-Test.

The generality (and weakness) of the generate-and-test scheme lies precisely in the fact that the generation process and the test process are completely independent [Newell and Simon 1972, p. 98].

GROUP-AND-DIFFERENTIATE

Group-and-Differentiate forms a list of plausible hypotheses and attempts to discriminate between them by exploiting the differences between the hypotheses.

HEURISTIC CLASSIFICATION

Clancey [1985] uses this term to describe systems that use Data Abstraction, Heuristic Association, and refinement to relate data to pre-enumerated solutions. Data Abstraction is also defined in the glossary, and Heuristic Association is defined in the text.

In simple classification, data may directly match solution features or may match after being abstracted. In heuristic classification, solutions and solution features may also be matched *heuristically*, by direct, non-hierarchical association with some concept in *another* classification hierarchy. For example, MYCIN does more than identify an unknown organism in terms of visible features of an organism: MYCIN heuristically relates an abstract characterization of the patient to a classification of diseases [Clancey 1985, p. 294].

HEURISTIC SEARCH

A technique for state space searching, with the **state space**...represented as a graph. It uses domain–specific knowledge expressed as a numerical **evaluation function** which assigns a number to each node of the graph. At each stage of the search, heuristic search develops the tip node with the best numeric score. Tip nodes may be stored on an **agenda** in order of numeric score [Bundy 1984, p. 46].
— Copyright 1984, Springer-Verlag Heidelberg. Reprinted by permission.

HIERARCHICAL GENERATE-AND-TEST

See "Generate-and-Test."

HORN CLAUSES

Horn Clauses are formulae of first order **predicate calculus**...of the form

A1 & A2 & ... & An → A   or   A1 & A2 & ... & An →

where each of the Ai and A are atomic formulae i.e., of the form R(C1,...,Cn), where R is a **relation**, each Cj is a **term**, and $n \geq 0$.

They have several important properties when viewed from **mathematical logic**. ...In addition, they form the basis for the **logic programming language PROLOG**...: each predicate in a Prolog program has a horn clause definition. The above formulae would be written

A :– A1, A2,..., An   and   ?– A1, A2,... An

respectively as Prolog programs [Bundy 1984, p. 48].
— Copyright 1984, Springer-Verlag Heidelberg. Reprinted by permission.

INTERMEDIATE HYPOTHESES

Conclusions that are not generally acceptable as final answers but help narrow down the possibilities to a restricted range. Typically they involve general descriptions, such as "upper-respiratory infection," that are consistent with a number of conclusions.

LEAST COMMITMENT

Instead of choosing values for the variables, it [MOLGEN] formulates a constraint on their values that can be taken into account in a later constraint satisfaction step. ...This deferring of decisions until necessary is part of a least-commitment approach to problem-solving [pp. 121–122].
— Stefik, M. Planning with constraints (MOLGEN: Part 1). *Artificial Intelligence*, *16*, 111–139 (1981a). Copyright 1981, Elsevier Science Publishers B.V.

LINEAR INPUT STRATEGY

When this strategy is used, the choice of what to resolve with what at any time is restricted as follows. We start with the goal statement and resolve

it with one of the hypotheses to give a new clause. Then we resolve that with one of the hypotheses to give another new clause. Then we resolve that with one of the hypotheses, and so on. At each stage, we resolve the clause last obtained with one of the original hypotheses. At no point do we either use a clause that has been derived previously or resolve together two of the hypotheses [Clocksin and Mellish 1987, p. 237].
— Copyright 1987, Springer-Verlag New York. Reprinted by permission.

MATCH

Using the Match procedure requires writing a set of conditions for each decision-making rule that ensure that all of the items of information are available that are required to make the decision with complete confidence. To simplify writing these conditions, an ordering of decision steps is developed and decision rules are made contingent on having reached the point in the ordering where most of their requirements have already been satisfied.

Basically the method [Match] is applicable if it is possible to order a set of decisions in such a way that no decision has to be made until the information sufficient for making that decision is available. This applicability condition is trivially satisfied if the set of decisions required by a task is fixed and can be ordered a priori. But in the VAX-11/780 configuration task, the set of decisions varies widely from configuration to configuration. The Match method is a procedure for dynamically ordering a set of decisions. When Match is used, each decision brings one closer to the successful completion of the task [p. 40].
— McDermott, J. R1: A rule-based configurer of computer systems. *Artificial Intelligence, 19,* 39–88 (1982). Copyright 1982, Elsevier Science Publishers B.V.

McDermott [1982, pp. 54f.] shows how his use of the term "Match" is consistent with the original formulation of the term by Newell [1973, pp. 20–21]. This discussion may be easier to understand if the following string matching problem is viewed as the simplest instance of Match: Compare the form $av_1v_1v_2dv_2$ with the string $abbcdg$. The items v_1 and v_2 in the form are variables, so if b is substituted for v_1 and c is substituted for v_2, then the two forms match until g is reached. At this point the match fails, and there is no point to backtracking as there was only one possible choice for each decision made earlier in the matching process.

MEANS–ENDS ANALYSIS

A technique for controlling search. Given a current state and a goal state, an operator is chosen which will reduce the difference between the two. This operator is applied to the current state to produce a new state, and the process is recursively applied to this new state and the goal state [Bundy 1984, p. 70].
— Copyright 1984, Springer-Verlag Heidelberg. Reprinted by permission.

MODEL-DRIVEN REASONING

By *model-driven* we mean "based on expectation" where the expectation is inferred from knowledge of the domain [Nii, Feigenbaum, Anton, and Rockmore 1982].
— Reprinted with permission from *AI Magazine*, 1982, p. 35, published by the American Association for Artificial Intelligence.

MULTIPLE LEVELS OF DETAIL

We will use an example from the expert system ABEL to illustrate multiple levels of detail. The ABEL system represents the fact that diarrhea causes dehydration at the clinical level of detail. At the next level of detail that causal connection is expanded to show that diarrhea causes the loss of lower gastrointestinal fluid (lower GI loss) that results in dehydration. At the next level of detail the connection between lower GI loss and dehydration is expanded to show that lower GI loss leads to sodium loss and water loss that produce dehydration. Two other expert systems that use multiple levels of detail are HEARSAY-II and CRYSALIS.

MULTIPLE VIEWS

The SYN system [de Kleer and Sussman 1980] is a circuit synthesis program that uses different points of view when reasoning about a circuit. For example, SYN establishes both an ac and a dc (alternating and direct current) model of an amplifier. The same parameter may occur in both models, and constraints associated with the different models can be combined to provide a unique solution for a shared parameter.

OBJECT-ORIENTED PROGRAMMING

Object-oriented programming is the design principle, pioneered in SMALLTALK, that descriptive and procedural attributes of an object should be associated directly with that object. Object-oriented programming can thus be highly modular. Since each object has its own procedural characteristics, it can perform local actions such as display or modify itself, and it can both receive information from and return information to other objects [Kunz, Kehler, and Williams].
— Reprinted with permission from *AI Magazine*, 1984, p. 52, published by the American Association for Artificial Intelligence.

OPPORTUNISTIC SEARCH

Blackboards are often used in conjunction with opportunistic search; this is because Blackboards store pieces of a solution and opportunistic search decides, at any time, which partial solution to expand into a more complete solution. The HEARSAY-II program is an example of a system that does opportunistic search with a Blackboard. The first quote describes HEARSAY-II's opportunistic search strategy.

We refer to a system's ability to exploit selectively its best data and most promising methods as "opportunistic" problem solving [Nii and Feigenbaum 1978, Hayes-Roth and Hayes-Roth 1979]. Hearsay-II developed several mechanisms to support such opportunistic behavior. In particular, its focus policies and prioritized scheduling allocate computation resources first to those KSs [Knowledge Sources] that exploit the most credible hypotheses, promise the most significant increments to the solution, and use the most reliable and inexpensive methods [Erman, Hayes-Roth, Lesser, and Reddy 1980, p. 245].
— Copyright 1980, Association for Computing Machinery, Inc. Reprinted by permission.

Building a signal interpretation system within the program organization ...can best be described as *opportunistic* analysis. Bits and pieces of information must be used as the opportunity arises to build slowly a coherent picture of the world—much like putting a jigsaw puzzle together [Nii, Feigenbaum, Anton, and Rockmore 1982].
— Reprinted with permission from *AI Magazine*, 1982, p. 35, published by the American Association for Artificial Intelligence.

PARTIAL MATCHING

A partial-match is a comparison of two or more descriptions that identifies their similarities. Because typical descriptions are formulated as symbolic property-lists or propositional formulas, a partial-match of two descriptions includes three components: an *abstraction*, consisting of all properties or propositions common to both compared descriptions; and two *residual* terms, representing the properties that are true of only one or the other of the descriptions [Hayes-Roth 1978, p. 557].
— Copyright 1978, Academic Press. Reprinted by permission.

PREDICATE CALCULUS

Predicate calculus is a formal language in which it is possible to express statements about simple domains. It comprises a set of symbols, and rules for combining these into terms and formulae. There are also rules of **inference**, which state how a new formula can be derived from old formulae. A logical system will have an initial set of sentences (**"axioms"**) and any sentence which can be derived from these axioms using the inference rules is called a **"theorem"** of the system.

The standard logic is a well–defined notation in which exact descriptive statements can be formulated about any "model" (i.e., set of objects with relations between them). Moreover, purely formal manipulations of these symbolic statements (i.e., inference) can be used to produce further valid descriptions of that same model, without direct reference to the model itself.

Terms can be constants (names of objects), variables (marking which part of a formula is quantified) or functions applied to arguments (e.g. $f(a,b,x)$). Atomic sentences are formed by applying a predicate to a set argument term (e.g. $P(f(a,b,x), c, g(h(y)))$). Compound sentences can be formed by adding negation to a sentence (e.g. $\sim R(a,b)$), joining two statements with a **connective** such as $\wedge$ ("and"), $\vee$ ("or"), $\rightarrow$ ("implication").

There are two **quantifiers** which, used together with variables, allow the expression of universal statements:

$$(\forall x)Q(x): \quad \text{"for all x, Q(x)"}$$

and existential statements:

$$(\exists z)R(z,a): \quad \text{"there exists a z such that R(z,a)"}$$

Automatic inference techniques (e.g. resolution ...) for first-order logic have been widely explored [Bundy 1984, pp. 99–100].

— Copyright 1984, Springer-Verlag Heidelberg. Reprinted by permission.

PROCEDURAL ATTACHMENT

Attaching programs or procedures to data structures is called *procedural attachment*. Three kinds of procedural attachment are if-added, if-needed, and if-removed demons. Computing the voltage at a resistor's terminal after its current is measured and added to a data structure is an example of an if-added procedure. When a slot has a value that constantly changes, such as the position of a robotic vehicle, then instead of continually updating that value, an if-needed procedure can compute the position just when it is needed. If-removed procedures do computations after a slot has its value removed from the data structure.

PRUNING

The search for solutions to a problem is often organized as a search through a tree of candidate solutions. *Pruning* refers to eliminating entire branches of the tree from consideration.

Many ordinary problems, such as repairing a circuit or playing a game, may have search spaces of astronomical size. A problem solver may improve its efficiency by eliminating from consideration classes of candidate solutions that cannot succeed in the given case. People call this type of search reduction *pruning* [Hayes-Roth, F. 1984, p. 12].

RESOLUTION

Resolution is an important rule of inference that can be applied to a certain class of wffs [well-formed formulas] called *clauses*. A *clause* is defined as a wff consisting of a disjunction of literals. The resolution process, when it is applicable, is applied to a pair of *parent* clauses to produce a derived clause [p. 145].

The best way to obtain a general idea of the resolution inference rule is to understand how it applies to ground clauses. Suppose we have two ground clauses, $P1 \vee P2 \vee \cdots \vee PN$ and $\sim P1 \vee Q2 \vee \cdots QM$. We assume that all of the Pi and Qj are distinct. Note that one of these clauses contains a literal that is the exact negation of one of the literals in the other clause. From these two *parent* clauses we can infer a new clause, called the *resolvent* of the two. The resolvent is computed by taking the disjunction of the two clauses and then eliminating the complementary pair, $P1$, $\sim P1$ [i.e., the resolvent is $P2 \vee \cdots \vee PN \vee Q2 \vee \cdots \vee QM$] [Nilsson 1980, p. 149].

> — *Principles of Artificial Intelligence* © by Morgan Kaufmann Publishers. Reprinted by permission.

RULES

In summary, then, let us say what we mean by rule-based systems. They are expert systems whose primary mode of representation is simple conditional sentences; they are extensions of production systems in which the concepts are closer in grain size to concepts used by experts than to psychological concepts. Rule-based systems are deductively not as powerful as logical theorem-proving programs because their only rule of inference is *modus ponens* and their syntax allows only a subset of logically well-formed expressions to be clauses in conditional sentences. Their primary distinction from logic-based systems is that rules define facts in the context of how they will be used, while expressions in logic-based systems are intended to define facts independently of their use.

Rule-based systems are primarily distinguished from frame-based systems by their restricted syntax. The emphasis in a rule is on the inferential relationship between facts (for example, "A is evidence for B" or "A causes B"). In a frame the emphasis is on characterizing concepts by using links of many types (including evidential relations).

Rule-based systems are sometimes characterized as "shallow" reasoning systems in which rules encode no causal knowledge. While this is largely (but not entirely) true of MYCIN, it is not a necessary feature of rule-based systems [Buchanan and Shortliffe 1984, p. 672].

> — Buchanan/Shortliffe, *Rule-Based Expert Systems*, © 1984 by B. G. Buchanan and E. H. Shortliffe. Reprinted with permission of Addison-Wesley Publishing Co., Inc., Reading, Massachusetts.

SCORING FUNCTIONS

Scoring functions rank hypotheses by giving each hypothesis credit for explaining observations or data. The score a hypothesis receives depends on the amount and importance of the data it explains. Fuzzy-Set Theory, EMYCIN Certainty Factors, Bayesian updating, and Dempster–Shafer Theory are all examples of scoring functions. A variety of ad hoc schemes have also been employed for many of the same purposes.

SEMANTIC NETWORKS

A method of knowledge representation where objects or concepts are represented by nodes in a graph and relationships between those objects or concepts are represented by arcs connecting the nodes. Arcs labeled *is-a* and *has-part* are frequently used to define relationships between concepts. For example, *Canary is-a bird* and *Bird has-part wing*.

SUBJECTIVE BAYESIAN METHODS

Sometimes it is not possible or convenient to use statistical estimates of probabilities when performing Bayes Rule computations. Subjective Bayesian Methods rely on getting experts to provide a subjective estimate of some of the probabilities. (See Duda, Hart, and Nilsson [1976] for a discussion of the use of Subjective Bayesian Methods in expert systems.)

TAXONOMIES

A hierarchical representation that describes the relationships between classes and subclasses.

TOP–DOWN REFINEMENT

Top–down refinement tailors an abstraction to fit each problem. The following aspects of the approach are important: .... The problem solution proceeds from the top downward, that is, from the most abstract to the most specific. Solutions to the problem are completed at one level before moving down to the next more specific level [Hayes-Roth, Waterman, and Lenat 1983, pp. 104–105].
— Hayes-Roth/Waterman/Lenat, *Building Expert Systems*, © 1983, Addison-Wesley Publishing Co., Inc., Reading, Massachusetts. Reprinted with permission.

TRUTH MAINTENANCE SYSTEMS

I have borrowed the term truth maintenance system (TMS) from Jon Doyle to describe any system with the following four characteristics:

(a) It performs some form of propositional deduction from a set of premises.

(b) It maintains justifications and explains the results of its deductions.

(c) It incrementally updates its beliefs when premises are added or removed.

(d) It does dependency-directed backtracking; i.e., when a contradiction arises it uses the recorded justifications to track down the premises which underlie that contradiction.

[McAllester 1980, p. 1].
  — Copyright 1980, Massachusetts Institute of Technology. Reprinted by permission.

APPENDIX B

References

Adams, J. B. A probability model of medical reasoning and the MYCIN model. *Mathematical Biosciences*, *32*, 177–186 (1976). Reprinted in *Rule-Based Expert Systems: The MYCIN Experiments of the Stanford Heuristic Programming Project*, B. G. Buchanan and E. H. Shortliffe (eds.). Reading, MA: Addison-Wesley, 1984, pp. 263–271.

Aiello, N. A comparative study of control strategies for expert systems: AGE implementation of three variations of PUFF. *Proceedings of the National Conference on Artificial Intelligence (AAAI-83)*, Washington, DC, 1983, pp. 1–4.

Aikins, J. *Prototypes and Production Rules: A Knowledge Representation for Computer Consultations*. Ph.D. thesis, Stanford University, 1980.

Aikins, J. S., Kunz, J. C., Shortliffe, E. H., and Fallat, R. J. PUFF: An expert system for interpretation of pulmonary function data. *Computers and Biomedical Research*, *16*, 199–208 (1983).

Allen, J. F. *Maintaining Knowledge about Temporal Intervals*. Technical Report 86, University of Rochester, January 1981 (1981a).

Allen, J. F. *A General Model of Action and Time*. Technical Report 97, University of Rochester, November 1981 (1981b).

Andress, K. M., and Kak, A. C. Evidence accumulation and flow of control in a hierarchical spatial reasoning system. *AI Magazine*, *9* (2), 75–94 (1988).

Baker, P. L., and Smoliar, S. W. Applying artificial intelligence to the interpretation of petroleum well logs. *The First Conference on Artificial Intelligence Applications*, IEEE Computer Society, 1984, pp. 558–561.

Barnett, J. Some issues of control in expert systems. *Proceedings of the International Conference on Cybernetics and Society*, Seattle, WA, October, 1982, pp. 1–5.

Barr, A., and Feigenbaum, E. A. (eds.), *The Handbook of Artificial Intelligence*, Vol. 1, Palo Alto, CA: Morgan Kaufmann, 1981.

Bennett, J. S. ROGET: Acquiring the conceptual structure of a diagnostic expert system. *IEEE Workshop on Knowledge-Based Systems*, Denver, 1984, pp. 83–88.

Bennett, J. S. ROGET: A knowledge-based consultant for acquiring the conceptual structure of a diagnostic expert system. *Journal of Automated Reasoning*, *1*, 49–74 (1985).

Bennett, J. S., and Engelmore, R. S. Experience using EMYCIN. In *Pergamon–Infotech State of the Art Report on Machine Intelligence*. Maidenhead, Berkshire, U.K.: Infotech Ltd., 1981. Reprinted in *Rule-Based Expert Systems: The MYCIN Experiments of the Stanford Heuristic Programming Project*, B. G. Buchanan and E. H. Shortliffe (eds.). Reading, MA: Addison-Wesley, 1984, pp. 314–328.

Bobrow, D. G., and Winograd, T. An overview of KRL, a knowledge representation language. *Cognitive Science*, *1*, 3–46 (1977).

Brachman, R. J. "I lied about the trees" or, defaults and definitions in knowledge representation. *AI Magazine*, *6* (3), 80–93 (1985).

Brachman, R. J., Fikes, R. E., and Levesque, H. J. KRYPTON: Integrating terminology and assertion. *Proceedings of the National Conference on Artificial Intelligence (AAAI-83)*, Washington, DC, 1983, pp. 31–35 (1983a).

Brachman, R. J., Fikes, R. E., and Levesque, H. J. KRYPTON: A functional approach to knowledge representation. *Computer*, *16*, (October) 67–73 (1983b).

Brooks, R., and Heiser, J. Some experience with transferring the MYCIN system to a new domain. *IEEE Transactions on Pattern Analysis and Machine Intelligence*, *PAMI-2*, 477–478 (1980).

Brown, J. S., Burton, R. R., and de Kleer, J. Pedagogical, natural language and knowledge engineering techniques in SOPHIE I, II, and III. In *Intelligent Tutoring Systems*, D. Sleeman and J. S. Brown (eds.). New York: Academic Press, 1982, pp. 227–282.

Bruce, B. C. A model for temporal references and its application in a question answering program. *Artificial Intelligence*, *3*, 1–25 (1972).

Buchanan, B. G. Mechanizing the search for explanatory hypotheses. In *PSA 1982*, Vol. 2, P. D. Asquith and T. Nickles (eds.). East Lansing, MI: Philosophy of Science Association, 1983.

Buchanan, B. G., and Feigenbaum, E. A. DENDRAL and Meta-DENDRAL: Their applications dimension. *Artificial Intelligence*, *11*, 5–24 (1978). Reprinted in *Readings in Artificial Intelligence*, B. L. Webber and N. J. Nilsson (eds.). Palo Alto, CA: Morgan-Kaufmann, 1981.

Buchanan, B. G., and Shortliffe, E. H. (eds.), *Rule-Based Expert Systems: The MYCIN Experiments of the Stanford Heuristic Programming Project*. Reading, MA: Addison-Wesley, 1984.

Buchanan, B. G., Sutherland, G., and Feigenbaum, E. A. Rediscovering some problems of artificial intelligence in the context of organic chemistry. In *Machine Intelligence 5*, B. Meltzer and D. Michie (eds.), Edinburgh, U.K.: Edinburgh University Press, 1970.

Bundy, A. (ed.). *Catalogue of Artificial Intelligence Tools*. Berlin: Springer-Verlag, 1984.

Carbonell, J. R. AI in CAI: An artificial intelligence approach to computer-assisted instruction. *IEEE Transactions on Man–Machine Systems, MMS-11*, 190–202 (1970a).

Carbonell, J. R. *Mixed-Initiative Man–Computer Instructional Dialogues*. Report No. 1971, Bolt Beranek and Newman, Cambridge, MA, (1970b).

Chandrasekaran, B., and Mittal, S. Deep versus compiled knowledge approaches to diagnostic problem solving. *Proceedings of the National Conference on Artificial Intelligence (AAAI-82)*, Pittsburgh, PA, 1982, pp. 349–354.

Clancey, W. J. Tutoring rules for guiding a case method dialogue. *International Journal of Man–Machine Studies, 11* (1979). Reprinted in D. Sleeman and J. S. Brown (eds.), *Intelligent Tutoring Systems*. New York: Academic Press, 1982.

Clancey, W. J. The advantages of abstract control knowledge in expert systems design. *Proceedings of the National Conference on Artificial Intelligence (AAAI-83)*, Washington, DC, 1983, pp. 74–78 (1983a).

Clancey, W. J. Extensions to rules for explanation and tutoring. *Artificial Intelligence, 20*, 215–251 (1983). Reprinted in *Rule-Based Expert Systems: The MYCIN Experiments of the Stanford Heuristic Programming Project*, B. G. Buchanan and E. H. Shortliffe (eds.). Reading, MA: Addison-Wesley, 1984, pp. 531–568 (1983b).

Clancey, W. J. Heuristic classification. *Artificial Intelligence, 27*, 289–350 (1985).

Clancey, W. J. *Knowledge-Based Tutoring: The GUIDON Program*. Cambridge, MA: MIT Press, 1987.

Clancey, W. J., and Shortliffe, E. H. (eds.). *Readings in Medical Artificial Intelligence: The First Decade*. Reading, MA: Addison-Wesley, 1984.

Clocksin, W. F., and Mellish, C. S. *Programming in Prolog*, 3rd ed. New York: Springer-Verlag, 1987.

Cohen, P. R. *Heuristic Reasoning about Uncertainty: An Artificial Intelligence Approach*. Ph.D. thesis, Stanford University, 1983.

Conan Doyle, A. The adventure of the beryl coronet. In *The Adventures of Sherlock Holmes*, Harper & Bros., 1892.

Cumberpatch, J., and Heaps, H. S. A disease-conscious method for sequential diagnosis by use of disease probabilities without assumption of symptom independence. *International Journal of Biomedical Computing*, 7, 61–78 (1976).

Davis, P. R., and Chien, R. T. Using and reusing partial plans. *Proceedings of the Fifth International Joint Conference on Artificial Intelligence*, Cambridge, MA, 1977, p. 494.

Davis, R. *Applications of Meta-Level Knowledge to the Construction, Maintenance, and Use of Large Knowledge Bases.* Report AIM-283, Stanford University, 1976.

Davis, R. Meta-rules: Reasoning about control. *Artificial Intelligence*, 15, 179–222 (1980).

Davis, R. Diagnostic reasoning based on structure and behavior. *Artificial Intelligence*, 24, 347–410 (1984).

Davis, R., and Buchanan, B. G. Meta-level knowledge: Overview and applications. *Proceedings of the Fifth International Joint Conference on Artificial Intelligence*, Cambridge, MA, 1977, pp. 920–927.

Davis, R., Buchanan, B. G., and Shortliffe, E. H. Production rules as a representation for a knowledge-based consultation program. *Artificial Intelligence*, 8, 15–45 (1977).

Davis, R., and King, J. J. *An Overview of Production Systems.* Computer Science Department, Stanford University (Stanford Report Nos. CS-STAN-CS-75-524 and AIM-271), October 1975. Reprinted in *Rule-Based Expert Systems: The MYCIN Experiments of the Stanford Heuristic Programming Project*, B. G. Buchanan and E. H. Shortliffe (eds.). Reading, MA: Addison-Wesley, 1984, pp. 20–52.

Davis, R., and Lenat, D. *Knowledge-Based Systems in Artificial Intelligence.* New York: McGraw-Hill, 1982.

Davis, R., and Shrobe, H. Representing structure and behavior of digital hardware. *Computer*, 16, 75–81 (October 1983).

de Kleer, J. Choices without backtracking. *Proceedings of the National Conference on Artificial Intelligence (AAAI-84)*, Austin, TX, 1984, pp. 79–85.

de Kleer, J. An assumption-based TMS. *Artificial Intelligence*, 28, 127–162 (1986).

de Kleer, J., and Sussman, G. J. Propagation of constraints applied to circuit synthesis. *Circuit Theory and Applications*, 8, 127–144 (1980).

Duda, R. O., Hart, P. E., and Nilsson, N. J. Subjective Bayesian methods for rule-based inference systems. *Proceedings of the National Computer Conference*, 1976, pp. 1075–1081.

Duda, R. O., Hart, P. E., Barrett, P., Gaschnig, J., Konolige, K., Reboh, R., and Slocum, J. *Development of the PROSPECTOR Consultant System for Mineral Exploration.* Final report for SRI Projects 5821 and 6415, Artificial Intelligence Center, SRI International, 1978.

Duda, R., Gaschnig, J., and Hart, P. Model design in the Prospector consultant system for mineral exploration. In *Expert Systems in the Micro-electronic Age*, D. Michie (ed.). Edinburgh, U.K.: Edinburgh University Press, 1979.

Durfee, E. H., and Lesser, V. R. Incremental planning to control a blackboard-based problem solver. *Proceedings of the National Conference on Artificial Intelligence (AAAI-86)*, Philadelphia, PA, 1986, pp. 58–64.

Dworkin, R. Hard cases. *Harvard Law Review, 88*, 1057–1109 (1975).

Engleman, C., Scarl, E., and Berg, C. Interactive frame instantiation. *Proceedings of the National Conference on Artificial Intelligence (AAAI-80)*, Stanford, CA, 1980, pp. 184–186.

Engelmore, R. S., and Terry, A. The structure and function of the CRYSALIS system. *Proceedings of the Sixth International Joint Conference on Artificial Intelligence*, Tokyo, Japan, 1979, pp. 250–256.

Erman, L. D., Hayes-Roth, F., Lesser, V. R., and Reddy, D. R. The Hearsay-II speech understanding system: Integrating knowledge to resolve uncertainty. *Computing Surveys, 12*, 213–253 (1980).

Erman, L. D., London, P. E., and Fickas, S. F. The design and example use of Hearsay-III. *Proceedings of the Seventh International Joint Conference on Artificial Intelligence*, Vancouver, BC, 1981, pp. 409–415.

Ernst, G., and Newell, A. *GPS: A Case Study in Generality and Problem Solving*. New York: Academic Press, 1969.

Fagan, L. M., Kunz, J. C., Feigenbaum, E. A., and Osborn, J. J. Extensions to the rule-based formalism for a monitoring task. In *Rule-Based Expert Systems: The MYCIN Experiments of the Stanford Heuristic Programming Project*, B. G. Buchanan and E. H. Shortliffe (eds.). Reading, MA: Addison-Wesley, 1984, pp. 397–423.

Fagan, L. M., Shortliffe, E. H., and Buchanan, B. G. Computer-based medical decision making: From MYCIN to VM. In *Automedica, 3*, 97–106 (1980). Reprinted in *Readings in Medical Artificial Intelligence: The First Decade*, W. J. Clancey and E. H. Shortliffe (eds.). Reading, MA: Addison-Wesley, 1984, pp. 241–255.

Feigenbaum, E. A. The art of artificial intelligence: I. Themes and case studies of knowledge engineering. *Proceedings of the Fifth International Joint Conference on Artificial Intelligence*, 1977, pp. 1014–1049. Reprinted in *Expert Systems in the Micro-electronic Age*, D. Michie (ed.). Edinburgh, U.K.: Edinburgh University Press, 1979.

Feltovich, P. J., Johnson, P. E., Moller, J. H., and Swanson, D. B. LCS: The role and development of medical knowledge in diagnostic expertise. In *Readings in Medical Artificial Intelligence: The First Decade*, W. J. Clancey and E. H. Shortliffe (eds.). Reading, MA: Addison-Wesley, 1984, pp. 275–319.

Fikes, R. E., and Nilsson, N. STRIPS: A new approach to the application of theorem proving to problem solving. *Artificial Intelligence, 2*, 189–208 (1971).

Fikes, R., and Hendrix, G. A network-based knowledge representation and its natural deduction system. *Proceedings of the Fifth International Joint Conference on Artificial Intelligence*, Cambridge, MA, 1977, pp. 235–246.

Finin, T., McAdams, J., and Kleinosky, P. FOREST—an expert system for automatic test equipment. *The First Conference on Artificial Intelligence Applications*, IEEE Computer Society, 1984, pp. 350–356.

Firby, R. J. An investigation into reactive planning in complex domains. *Proceedings of the National Conference on Artificial Intelligence (AAAI-87)*, Seattle, WA, 1987, pp. 202–206.

Fox, M. Reasoning with incomplete knowledge in a resource-limited environment: Integrating reasoning and knowledge acquisition. *Proceedings of the Seventh International Joint Conference on Artificial Intelligence*, Vancouver, BC, 1981, pp. 313–318.

Fox, M. S. *Constraint-Directed Search: A Case Study of Job-Shop Scheduling.* Ph.D. dissertation, Computer Science Department, Carnegie-Mellon University, Pittsburgh, PA, 1983. (Available as Technical Report CMU-RI-TR-83-22 from The Robotics Institute, Carnegie-Mellon University.)

Fox, M. S., and Smith, S. F. *Constraint-Based Scheduling in an Intelligent Logistics Support System: An Artificial Intelligence Approach.* Annual Report, AFOSR Contract No. F49620-82-K-0017, July 1983.

Fox, M. S., Allen, B. P., Smith, S. F., and Strohm, G. A. *ISIS: A Constraint-Directed Reasoning Approach to Job Shop Scheduling.* Technical Report CMU-RI-TR-83-8, The Robotics Institute, Carnegie-Mellon University, Pittsburgh, PA, 1983.

Friedland, P., and Iwasaki, Y. The concept and implementation of skeletal plans. *Journal of Automated Reasoning*, *1*, 161–208 (1985).

Frost, R. *Introduction to Knowledge Base Systems.* New York: Macmillan, 1986.

Fukumori, K. *Fundamental Scheme for Train Scheduling (Application of Range-Constriction Search).* AI Memo 596, MIT Artificial Intelligence Laboratory, September 1980.

Gaines, B. R. Foundations of fuzzy reasoning. *International Journal of Man–Machine Studies*, *8*, 623–668 (1976).

Gasden, J. A. An expert system for evaluating electronic warfare tasking plans for the Royal Navy. *The First Conference on Artificial Intelligence Applications*, IEEE Computer Society, Denver, 1984, pp. 86–91.

Genesereth, M. Diagnosis using hierarchical design models. *Proceedings of the National Conference on Artificial Intelligence (AAAI-82)*, Pittsburgh, PA, 1982, pp. 278–283.

Genesereth, M. An overview of meta-level architecture. *Proceedings of the National Conference on Artificial Intelligence (AAAI-83)*, Washington, DC, 1983, pp. 119–124.

Genesereth, M. R., and Ginsberg, M. Logic programming. *Communications of the ACM*, *28* (9), 933–941 (1985).

Georgeff, M. P., and Lansky, A. Reactive reasoning and planning. *Proceedings of the National Conference on Artificial Intelligence (AAAI-87)*, Seattle, WA, 1987, pp. 677–682.

Gerring, P. E., Shortliffe, E. H., and van Melle, W. The Interviewer/Reasoner model: An approach to improving system responsiveness in interactive AI systems. *AI Magazine, 3* (4), 24–27 (1982).

Goldstein, I. P., and Roberts, R. B. NUDGE: A knowledge-based scheduling program. *Proceedings of the Fifth International Joint Conference on Artificial Intelligence*, Cambridge, MA, 1977, pp. 257–263.

Gordon, J., and Shortliffe, E. H. A method for managing evidential reasoning in a hierarchical hypothesis space. *Artificial Intelligence, 26*, 323–357 (1985).

Hart, H. L. A. *The Concept of Law.* Oxford, U.K.: Clarendon Press, 1961.

Hayes, C. Using goal interactions to guide planning. *Proceedings of the National Conference on Artificial Intelligence (AAAI-87)*, Seattle, WA, 1987, pp. 224–228.

Hayes-Roth, B., and Hayes-Roth, F. A cognitive model of planning. *Cognitive Science, 3*, 275–310 (1979).

Hayes-Roth, F. The knowledge-based expert system: A tutorial. *Computer, 17* (9), 11–28 (September 1984).

Hayes-Roth, F. The role of partial and best matches in knowledge systems. In *Pattern-Directed Inference Systems*, D. A. Waterman and F. Hayes-Roth (eds.), New York: Academic Press, 1978, pp. 557–576.

Hayes-Roth, F., and Lesser, V. R. Focus of attention in the Hearsay-II system. *Proceedings of the Fifth International Joint Conference on Artificial Intelligence*, Cambridge, MA, 1977, pp. 27–35.

Hayes-Roth, F., Waterman, D. A., and Lenat, D. B. (eds.), *Building Expert Systems*. Reading, MA: Addison-Wesley, 1983.

Heloise. *Hints from Heloise.* New York: Avon, 1980.

Horowitz, E., and Sahni, S. *Fundamentals of Computer Algorithms.* Rockville, MD: Computer Science Press, 1978.

Horvitz, E. J., Heckerman, D. E., Nathwani, B. N., and Fagan, L. M. Diagnostic strategies in the hypothesis-directed PATHFINDER system. *The First Conference on Artificial Intelligence Applications*, IEEE Computer Society, Denver, 1984, pp. 630–636.

Jelliffe, R. W. An improved method of digoxin therapy. *Annals of Internal Medicine, 69*, 703–717 (1968).

Jelliffe, R. W., Buell, J., and Kalaba, R. A computer program for digitalis dosage regimens. *Mathematical Biosciences, 9*, 179–193 (1970).

Jelliffe, R. W., Buell, J., and Kalaba, R. Reduction of digitalis toxicity by computer-assisted glycoside dosage regimens. *Annals of Internal Medicine, 77*, 891–906 (1972).

Kahn, G. On when diagnostic systems want to do without causal knowledge. In *ECAI-84: Advances in Artificial Intelligence*, T. O'Shea (ed.). Amsterdam: Elsevier, 1984, pp. 21–30.

Kahn, G. MORE: From observing knowledge engineers to automating knowledge engineering. In *Automating Knowledge Acquisition for Expert Systems*, S. Marcus (ed.). Boston, MA: Kluwer, 1988.

Kahn, G., and McDermott, J. The MUD system. *The First Conference on Artificial Intelligence Applications*, IEEE Computer Society, Denver, 1984, pp. 116–122.

Kahn, G., Nowlan, S., and McDermott, J. A foundation for knowledge acquisition. In *IEEE Workshop on Knowledge-Based Systems*. Denver, 1984, p. 89–96.

Kahn, K., and Gorry, G. A. Mechanizing temporal knowledge. *Artificial Intelligence*, *9*, 87–108 (1977).

Klahr, P., McArthur, D., and Narain, S. SWIRL: An object-oriented air battle simulator. *Proceedings of the National Conference on Artificial Intelligence (AAAI-82)*, Pittsburgh, PA, 1982, pp. 331–334.

Kline, P. J., and Dolins, S. B. *Choosing Architectures for Expert Systems*. Final Technical Report RADC-TR-85-192, October 1985, Rome Air Development Center, Griffiss AFB, New York 13441. (Available from the National Technical Information Service; access no. AD A163343.)

Kline, P. J., and Dolins, S. B. Problem features that influence the design of expert systems. *Proceedings of the National Conference on Artificial Intelligence (AAAI-86)*, Philadelphia, PA, 1986, pp. 956–962.

Knuth, D. E. *The Art of Computer Programming*, Vol. 1: Fundamental Algorithms. Reading, MA: Addison-Wesley, 1968.

Koton, P. *A System to Aid in the Solution of Problems in Molecular Genetics*. SM thesis, MIT Laboratory for Computer Science, May 1983.

Koton, P. *Towards a Problem Solving System for Molecular Genetics*. Technical Report 338, MIT Laboratory for Computer Science, Cambridge, MA, 1985 (1985a).

Koton, P. A. Empirical and model-based reasoning in expert systems. *Proceedings of the Ninth International Joint Conference on Artificial Intelligence*, 1985, pp. 297–299 (1985b).

Kowalski, R. *Logic for Problem Solving*. New York: Elsevier, 1979.

Kulikowski, C. A. Artificial intelligence methods and systems for medical consultation. *IEEE Transactions on Pattern Analysis and Machine Intelligence*, *PAMI-2* (5), 464–476 (1980).

Kunz, J., Shortliffe, E. H., Buchanan, B. G., and Feigenbaum, E. A. *Comparison of Techniques of Computer-Assisted Decision Making in Medicine*. Report No. HPP-83-32, Heuristic Programming Project, Stanford University, April 1983.

Kunz, J. C., Kehler, T. P., and Williams, M. D. Applications development using a hybrid AI development system. *AI Magazine*, *5* (3), 41–54 (1984).

Lenat, D. B. *AM: An Artificial Intelligence Approach to Discovery in Mathematics as Heuristic Search*. Ph.D. dissertation, Computer Science Department, Stanford University, 1976. (Stanford Report Nos. CS-STAN-76-570 and AIM-286. Reprinted with revisions in Davis and Lenat [1982].)

Lenat, D. B. Theory formation by heuristic search. The nature of heuristics II: Background and examples. *Artificial Intelligence*, *21*, 31–59 (1983).

Lenat, D. B., and Harris, G. Designing a rule system that searches for scientific discoveries. In *Pattern-Directed Inference Systems*, D. A. Waterman and F. Hayes-Roth (eds.). New York: Academic Press, 1978.

Lenat, D., Davis, R., Doyle, J., Genesereth, M., Goldstein, I., and Shrobe, H. Reasoning about reasoning. In *Building Expert Systems*, F. Hayes-Roth, D. A. Waterman, and D. B. Lenat (eds.). Reading, MA: Addison-Wesley, 1983.

Lenat, D. B., Hayes-Roth, F., and Klahr, P. Cognitive economy in artificial intelligence systems. *Proceedings of the Sixth International Joint Conference on Artificial Intelligence*, Tokyo, Japan, 1979, pp. 531–536.

Lesser, V. R., and Erman, L. D. A retrospective view of the Hearsay-II architecture. *Proceedings of the Fifth International Joint Conference on Artificial Intelligence*, 1977, pp. 790–800.

Levesque, H. J. *A Formal Treatment of Incomplete Knowledge Bases*. Technical Report No. 3, Fairchild Laboratory for Artificial Intelligence Research, Palo Alto, CA, 1982.

Levesque, H. J. A fundamental tradeoff in knowledge representation and reasoning. *Proceedings of the Fourth Conference of the Canadian Society for Computational Studies of Intelligence*, London, Ontario, 1984, pp. 141–152.

McAllester, D. A. *An Outlook on Truth Maintenance*. AI Memo No. 551, MIT Artificial Intelligence Laboratory, 1980.

McArthur, D., and Klahr, P. *The ROSS Language Manual*. N-1854-AF, The Rand Corporation, Santa Monica, CA, 1982.

McCarthy J. Some expert systems need common sense. *Annals of the New York Academy of Sciences*, *426*, 129–137 (1984).

McCarty, L. T., and Sridharan, N. S. The representation of an evolving system of legal concepts: II. Prototypes and deformations. *Proceedings of the Seventh International Joint Conference on Artificial Intelligence*, 1981, pp. 246–253.

McDermott, D. A temporal logic for reasoning about processes and plans. *Cognitive Science*, *6*, 101–155 (1982).

McDermott, D., and Brooks, R. ARBY: Diagnosis with shallow causal models. *Proceedings of the National Conference on Artificial Intelligence (AAAI-82)*, Pittsburgh, PA, 1982, pp. 370–372.

McDermott, J. R1: A rule-based configurer of computer systems. *Artificial Intelligence*, *19*, 39–88 (1982).

McDermott, J. Preliminary steps toward a taxonomy of problem-solving methods. In *Automating Knowledge Acquisition for Expert Systems*, S. Marcus (ed.). Boston, MA: Kluwer, 1988.

McDermott, J., and Forgy, C. Production system conflict resolution strategies. In *Pattern-Directed Inference Systems*, D. A. Waterman and F. Hayes-Roth (eds.). New York: Academic Press, 1978, pp. 177–199.

McDermott, J., and Steele, B. Extending a knowledge-based system to deal with ad hoc constraints. *Proceedings of the Seventh International Joint Conference on Artificial Intelligence*, 1981, Vancouver, BC, pp. 824–828.

Miller, P. B. *Strategy Selection in Medical Diagnosis*. Project MAC Report No. TR-153, MIT, 1975.

Miller, R. A., Pople, H. E., Jr., and Myers, J. D. INTERNIST–1, an experimental computer-based diagnostic consultant for general internal medicine. *New England Journal of Medicine*, *307*, 468–476 (1982). Reprinted in *Readings in Medical Artificial Intelligence: The First Decade*, W. J. Clancey and E. H. Shortliffe (eds.). Reading, MA: Addison-Wesley, 1984, pp. 190–209.

Minsky, M. A framework for representing knowledge. In *The Psychology of Computer Vision*, P. H. Winston (ed.). New York: McGraw-Hill, 1975, pp. 211–277.

Mostow, J. Toward better models of the design process. *AI Magazine*, *6* (1), 44–57 (1985).

Newell, A. Artificial intelligence and the concept of mind. In *Computer Models of Thought and Language*, R. C. Schank and K. M. Colby (eds.). San Francisco: Freeman, 1973, pp. 1–60.

Newell, A., and Simon, H. A. *Human Problem Solving*. Englewood Cliffs, NJ: Prentice-Hall, 1972.

Nii, H. P. Blackboard systems: The blackboard model of problem solving and the evolution of blackboard architectures. *AI Magazine*, *7* (2), 38–64 (1986).

Nii, H. P., and Aiello, N. AGE (Attempt to Generalize): A knowledge-based program for building knowledge-based programs. *Proceedings of the Sixth International Joint Conference on Artificial Intelligence*, 1979, pp. 645–655.

Nii, H. P., and Feigenbaum, E. A. Rule-based understanding of signals. In *Pattern-Directed Inference Systems*, D. A. Waterman and F. Hayes-Roth (eds.). New York: Academic Press, 1978.

Nii, H. P., Feigenbaum, E. A., Anton, J. J., and Rockmore, A. J. Signal-to-symbol transformation: HASP/SIAP case study. *AI Magazine*, *3* (2), 23–35 (1982).

Nilsson, N. J. *Problem-Solving Methods in Artificial Intelligence*. New York: McGraw-Hill, 1971.

Nilsson, N. J. *Principles of Artificial Intelligence*. San Mateo, CA: Morgan Kaufmann Publishers, 1980.

Norusis, M. J., and Jacquez, J. A. Diagnosis. I. Symptom non-independence in mathematical models for diagnosis. *Computers in Biomedical Research, 8,* 156–172 (1975).

Patil, R. S. *Design of a Program for Expert Diagnosis of Acid Base and Electrolyte Disturbances.* TM–132, MIT Laboratory for Computer Science, 1979.

Patil, R. S. *Causal Representation of Patient Illness for Electrolyte and Acid–Base Diagnosis.* Ph.D. thesis, MIT, 1981. Technical Report MIT/LCS/TR-267, Laboratory of Computer Science, MIT.

Patil, R. S., Szolovits, P., and Schwartz, W. B. Causal understanding of patient illness in medical diagnosis. *Proceedings of the Seventh International Joint Conference on Artificial Intelligence,* 1981, pp. 893–899.

Pauker, S. G., Gorry, G. A., Kassirer, J. P., and Schwartz, W. B. Towards the simulation of clinical cognition: Taking a present illness by computer. *American Journal of Medicine, 60,* 981–996 (1976). Reprinted in *Readings in Medical Artificial Intelligence: The First Decade,* W. J. Clancey, and E. H. Shortliffe (eds.). Reading, MA: Addison-Wesley, 1984, pp. 131–159.

Pearl, J. *Probabilistic Reasoning in Intelligent Systems: Networks of Plausible Inference.* Palo Alto, CA: Morgan Kaufmann, 1988.

Pentland, A. P., and Fischler, M. A. A more rational view of logic or, up against the wall, logic imperialists. *AI Magazine, 4* (4), 15–18 (1983).

Pople, H. E., Jr. The formation of composite hypotheses in diagnostic problem solving: An exercise in synthetic reasoning. *Proceedings of the Fifth International Joint Conference on Artificial Intelligence,* Cambridge, MA, 1977, pp. 1030–1037.

Pople, H. E., Jr. Heuristic methods for imposing structure on ill-structured problems: The structuring of medical diagnostics. In *Artificial Intelligence in Medicine,* P. Szolovits (ed.). Boulder, CO: Westview Press, American Association for the Advancement of Science, 1982, pp. 119–190.

Pople, H. E., Myers, J. D., and Miller, R. A. DIALOG: A model of diagnostic logic for internal medicine. *Proceedings of the Fourth International Joint Conference on Artificial Intelligence,* Tbilisi, Georgia, U.S.S.R., 1975, pp. 848–855.

Reggia, J. A., Nau, D. S., and Wang, P. Y. A new inference method for frame-based expert systems. *Proceedings of the National Conference on Artificial Intelligence (AAAI-83),* Washington, DC, 1983, pp. 333–337.

Reggia, J. A., Nau, D. S., and Wang, P. Y. Diagnostic expert systems based on a set covering method. In *Developments in Expert Systems,* M. J. Coombs, (ed.). New York: Academic Press, 1984.

Rolston, D. W. A multiparadigm knowledge-based system for diagnosis of large mainframe peripherals. *The Third Conference on Artificial Intelligence Applications,* IEEE Computer Society, 1987, pp. 150–155.

Rosenschein, J. S., and Singh, V. *The Utility of Meta-Level Effort*. Report No. HPP-83-20, Heuristic Programming Project, Stanford University, March 1983.

Sacerdoti, E. D. Planning in a hierarchy of abstraction spaces. *Artificial Intelligence*, 5, 115–135 (1974).

Sacerdoti, E. D. *A Structure For Plans and Behavior*. New York: Elsevier North-Holland, 1977.

Schmolze, J. G., and Brachman, R. J. *Proceedings of the 1981 KL-ONE Workshop*. Technical Report 4842, Bolt, Beranek and Newman Inc., Cambridge, MA, 1982. Also FLAIR TR-4, Fairchild Lab for AI Research.

Schmolze, J. G., and Lipkis, T. A. Classification in the KL-ONE knowledge representation system. *Proceedings of the Eighth International Joint Conference on Artificial Intelligence*, 1983, 330–332.

Scott, A. C., Clancey, W. J., Davis, R., and Shortliffe, E. H. Methods for generating explanations. *American Journal of Computational Linguistics*, Microfiche 62, 1977. Reprinted in *Rule-Based Expert Systems: The MYCIN Experiments of the Stanford Heuristic Programming Project*, B. G. Buchanan and E. H. Shortliffe (eds.). Reading, MA: Addison-Wesley, 1984, pp. 263–271.

Shafer, G. *A Mathematical Theory of Evidence*. Princeton, NJ: Princeton University Press, 1976.

Sherman, H. B. *A Comparative Study of Computer-Aided Clinical Diagnosis of Birth Defects*. Technical Report MIT/LCS/TR-283, Laboratory of Computer Science, MIT, 1981.

Shortliffe, E. H., and Buchanan, B. G. A model of inexact reasoning in medicine. *Mathematical Biosciences*, 23, 351–379 (1975).

Shortliffe, E. H., Buchanan, B. G., and Feigenbaum, E. A. Knowledge engineering for medical decision making: A review of computer-based clinical decision aids. *Proceedings of the IEEE*, 67 (9), 1207–1224 (September 1979).

Silverman, H. *A Digitalis Therapy Advisor*. Master's thesis, MIT, Laboratory for Computer Science, MIT/LCS/TR-143, 1974.

Slagle, J. R., Gaynor, M. W., and Halpern, E. J. An intelligent control strategy for computer consultation. *IEEE Transactions on Pattern Analysis and Machine Intelligence*, PAMI-6, 1984, pp. 129–136.

Smith, B. C. *A Proposal for a Computational Model of Anatomical and Physiological Reasoning*. Technical Memo MIT/AI/TM-493, Artificial Intelligence Laboratory, MIT, 1978.

Smith, D. E., and Clayton, J. E. A frame-based production system architecture. *Proceedings of the Eighth International Joint Conference on Artificial Intelligence*, 1983, pp. 154–156.

Smith, S. F. *Exploiting Temporal Knowledge to Organize Constraints*. Intelligent Systems Laboratory, The Robotics Institute, Carnegie-Mellon University, CMU-RI-TR-83-12, July 1983.

Stallman, R. M., and Sussman, G. J. Forward reasoning and dependency-directed backtracking in a system for computer-aided analysis. *Artificial Intelligence*, *9*, 135–196 (1977).

Stallman, R., Weinreb, D., and Moon, D. *Lisp Machine Manual*. MIT Artificial Intelligence Laboratory, 6th ed., June 1984.

Steele, G. L. *The Definition and Implementation of a Computer Programming Language Based on Constraints*. Ph.D. dissertation, MIT (Technical Report AI-TR-595), Cambridge, MA, 1980.

Stefik, M. Planning with constraints (MOLGEN: Part 1). *Artificial Intelligence*, *16*, 111–139 (1981a).

Stefik, M. Planning and meta-planning (MOLGEN: Part 2). *Artificial Intelligence*, *16*, 141–169 (1981b).

Stefik, M., Aikins, J., Balzer, R., Benoit, J., Birnbaum, L., Hayes-Roth, F., and Sacerdoti, E. The organization of expert systems, a tutorial. *Artificial Intelligence*, *18*, 135–173 (1982).

Sussman, G. J., and Steele, G. Constraints: A language for expressing almost hierarchical descriptions. *Artificial Intelligence*, *14*, 1–40 (1980).

Swartout, W. A digitalis therapy advisor with explanations. *Proceedings of the Fifth International Joint Conference on Artificial Intelligence*, 1977, pp. 819–825.

Swartout, W. *Explainable Expert Systems*. USC/Information Sciences Institute, Marina del Rey, CA, October 1983.

Swartout, W. R. Explaining and justifying expert consulting programs. *Proceedings of the Seventh International Joint Conference on Artificial Intelligence*, 1981, pp. 815–823. Reprinted in *Readings in Medical Artificial Intelligence: The First Decade*, W. J. Clancey and E. H. Shortliffe (eds.). Reading, MA: Addison-Wesley, 1984, pp. 382–398.

Szolovits, P., and Pauker, S. G. Categorical and probabilistic reasoning in medical diagnosis. *Artificial Intelligence*, *11*, 115–144 (1978). Reprinted in *Readings in Medical Artificial Intelligence: The First Decade*, W. J. Clancey and E. H. Shortliffe (eds.). Reading, MA: Addison-Wesley, 1984, pp. 210–240.

Thorndike, P., McArthur, D., and Cammarata, S. *AUTOPILOT: A Distributed Planner for Air Fleet Control*. Technical Note N-1731-ARPA, The Rand Corporation, Santa Monica, CA, July 1981.

van Melle, W., Scott, A. C., Bennett, J. S., and Peairs, M. *The EMYCIN Manual*. Report Nos. STAN-CS-81-885 and HPP-81-16, Department of Computer Science, Stanford University, Palo Alto, CA, 1981.

Vere, S. A. *Planning in Time: Windows and Durations for Activities and Goals*. Technical Report, Jet Propulsion Laboratory, Pasadena, CA, November 1981.

Vere, S. Planning in time: Windows and durations for activities and goals. *IEEE Transactions on Pattern Analysis and Machine Intelligence*, *PAMI-5*, 246–267 (1983).

Villain, M. B. A system for reasoning about time. *Proceedings of the National Conference on Artificial Intelligence (AAAI-82)*, Pittsburgh, PA, 1982, pp. 197–201.

Walters, J. R., and Nielsen, N. R. *Crafting Knowledge-Based Systems: Expert Systems Made Easy Realistic.* New York: Wiley-Interscience, 1988.

Waltz, D. Understanding line drawings of scenes with shadows. In *The Psychology of Computer Vision*, P. H. Winston (ed.). New York: McGraw-Hill, 1975.

Waterman, D. A. *A Guide to Expert Systems.* Reading, MA: Addison-Wesley, 1986.

Weiss, S. M., and Kulikowski, C. A. *A Practical Guide to Designing Expert Systems.* Totowa, NJ: Rowman & Allanheld, 1984.

Wilkens, D. E. Recovering from execution errors in SIPE. *Computational Intelligence, 1*, 33–45 (1985).

Winograd, T. Frame representations and the procedural/declarative controversy. In *Representation and Understanding: Studies in Cognitive Science*, D. G. Bobrow and A. Collins (eds.). New York: Academic Press, 1975.

Winston, P. *Artificial Intelligence.* Reading, MA: Addison-Wesley, 1977.

Woods, W. A. What's in a link: Foundations for semantic networks. In *Representation and Understanding: Studies in Cognitive Science*, D. G. Bobrow and A. Collins (eds.). New York: Academic Press, 1975.

Zadeh, L. A. Fuzzy sets. *Information and Control, 8*, 338–353 (1965).

Index